C000127627

ISLAMIC RESEARCH ASSOCIATION

SERIES, No. 6

THE BOOK OF TRUTHFULNESS
(KITĀB AL-ṢIDQ)

ISLAMIC RESEARCH ASSOCIATION SERIES

1. **Diwan of Khaki Khorasani.** Persian text, edited with an introduction by W. Ivanow. 1933. Price, cloth Rs 1-10 (Foreign, 3s 6d.)

2. **Two Early Ismaili Treatises (Haft Babi Baba Sayyidna** and **Matlubu'l-mu'minin)** by Nasiru'ddin Tusi. Persian Text, edited with an introduction by W. Ivanow. 1933. Price, cloth .. .. As. 14 (2s. 6d.)

3. **True Meaning of Religion (Risala dar Haqiqati Din),** by Shihabu'd-din Shah Persian text, with a complete English translation by W Ivanow. 1933. Price, cloth Re. 1-4 (3s.)

4. **Kalami Pir,** or **Haft Babi Sayyid Nasir.** Persian text, edited and translated into English by W Ivanow 1935. Price, cloth.. .. .. Rs. 6-8 (10s)

5. **Arabon ki Jahaz-rani (Arab Navigation),** by Syed Sulaiman Nadwi Urdu 1935. Price, cloth Re 1 (2s. 6d.)

6. **The Book of Truthfulness (Kitāb al-Ṣidq)** by Abū Saʿīd al-Kharrāz. Arabic text, edited and translated by A. J. Arberry. 1937 Price, cloth Rs 4 (6s.)

A Creed of- the Shi'ites, being a translation of the **Risalatu'l-i'tiqadati'l-Imamiyya** of Ibn Babuya, by Asaf A. A. Fyzee (in preparation).

OXFORD UNIVERSITY PRESS

ISLAMIC RESEARCH ASSOCIATION
No. 6

THE BOOK OF TRUTHFULNESS
(KITĀB AL-ṢIDQ)

BY

ABU SA'ID AL-KHARRAZ

Edited and translated from the Istanbul Unicum by

ARTHUR JOHN ARBERRY, LITT.D.

Assistant Librarian in the India Office
Formerly Fellow of Pembroke College, Cambridge

Published for the Islamic Research Association by
HUMPHREY MILFORD
OXFORD UNIVERSITY PRESS
LONDON   NEW YORK   BOMBAY
CALCUTTA   MADRAS
1937

PRINTED IN INDIA BY P. KNIGHT
BAPTIST MISSION PRESS
41A, LOWER CIRCULAR ROAD, CALCUTTA

PREFACE

Abū Saʿīd Ahmad ibn ʿĪsā al-Kharrāz was one of the best-known of the Baghdad school of Ṣūfīs, which flourished in the 3/9 century. As is the case unfortunately with most of his contemporaries in mysticism, little is known of his actual life, apart from the anecdotes illustrative of piety or supernatural gifts which the later compilers relate. Even the date of his death is a matter of the most extraordinary uncertainty. Among the years mentioned by various authorities are 247, 277, 279, 286 and 306.[1] Of these dates the year 247 is expressly ruled out as absurd[2]; the authority for 286 is Abū Saʿīd al-Mālīnī, who bases his statement on the information given by Abū 'l-Qāsim al-Nihāwandī, who was a pupil of Kharrāz for fourteen years, and therefore merits credence.[3] Kharrāz was an associate of Dhū 'l-Nūn al-Miṣrī, Bishr ibn al-Ḥārith, Sarī al-Saqaṭī, and al-Nibājī, well-known Ṣūfīs who figure in many of the anecdotes of which Kharrāz is the hero.

A masterly analysis of the doctrine and importance of Kharrāz has been written by L. Massignon,[4] and it is not proposed to add anything to this account here. The text now published and translated is the sole surviving work of Kharrāz,[5] though considerable fragments of his sayings and writings are preserved in the various Ṣūfī compendia, notably the *Kitāb al-Lumaʿ* of Sarrāj. The present work is cast in the form of a dialogue, and purports to consist of answers given to Kharrāz by an unnamed instructor. That this is a mere literary fiction is

---

[1] *Ta'rīkh Baghdād*, IV, p. 278; *al-Risālah al-Qushayrīyah* (Būlāq, 1284), p. 29; Ibn ʿAsākir, *al-Ta'rīkh al-kabīr*, I, p. 432; *al-Ṭabaqāt al-kubrā*, I, p. 107.

[2] *Ta'rīkh Baghdād, loc. cit.*

[3] *Ibid.* Cf. Massignon, *Essai*, p. 270, n. 3.

[4] *Op. cit.*, pp. 270–3; *Encyclopædia of Islām*, II, col. 969 b.

[5] Preserved in MS. Şehit Ali 1374.

clear, especially from the passages where it is stated that " this is all that can be mentioned in a book " [1] . no oral teacher would use such an expression

The importance of this treatise lies in the fact that, apart from the writings of Muhāsibī, it is the earliest systematic presentation of the theory of Sūfī experience, written by a practising Sūfī   Beginning with the idea of ṣidq or truthfulness, the author develops his theme to include the " stations " of fear, hope, trust, love, shame, longing, intimacy, all of which the mystic must pass on his path to God.   In a style which foreshadows the practice of later writers Kharrāz begins with Qur'ānic sanctions, follows these by references to the Sunna and the lives of the saints, and amplifies his discourse with sayings of pious men, frequently anonymous.   The constant insistence on the experience of the prophets and men of piety, particularly Muhammad himself, and the " agony " suffered by him, as an example to the Sūfī in his spiritual life, is most remarkable. Very striking also is the obviously authentic description of the effect of love of God in the mystic's heart.[2]   Finally the important question is proposed, does the mystic reach a stage in which he ceases consciously to strive after truthfulness ?   This question Kharrāz answers (in the mouth of his interlocutor) in a fashion which explains why he was held to have been the first to formulate the doctrine of fanā' and baqā' [3]   Throughout the discourse the author constantly refers, typically as a mystic, to higher degrees of the various stations which cannot be described in written language.

The genuineness of this tract has not been doubted by Massignon, who alone has studied it , and there is in fact some internal evidence which appears to set its authenticity beyond suspicion.[4]   It is not mentioned by name in any Sūfī or bibliographical authority,[5] but this is not necessarily surprising : only

---

[1] Cf. pp. 44, 49.   [2] P 45.

[3] Massignon, op. cit , pp. 271, 272, n. 1

[4] See pp 50, n. 3 ; 62, n. 1.

[5] A Kitāb al-Sirr is referred to, cf. Massignon loc. cit

one copy of the work has survived, and that by the hand of the well-known pupil of Ibn ʿArabī, Ismāʿīl ibn Sawdakīn (d. 646/ 1248), so that it is permissible to conjecture that the book was a guarded secret of the Ṣūfīs, who communicated it to one another privately, without divulging its contents to the general public.

The text as given by the copyist is good, though not free from errors, of which the most frequent is the commonly-met omission of the particle is in interrogative forms Ismāʿīl ibn Sawdakīn does not attempt to correct these errors, though he was doubtless conscious of them, so that they must be referred to the archetype on which he drew, and possibly to the author himself In no place, however, is the text obscure, or its meaning doubtful.[1] Kharrāz writes in a clear and unambiguous style, which contrasts very favourably with the preciosity of Junayd and the letter-writers. This makes it all the more likely that the book was intended for Ṣūfīs only, for the artificial style adopted by the Ṣūfīs in their letters is indubitably due to a desire to avoid suspicion of being unorthodox, in the event of their letters being opened.[2]

I am deeply indebted to Professor A J Wensinck for the great trouble he took in supplying me with references to the canonical collections of Traditions, for such traditions quoted in the *Kitāb al-Ṣidq* as occur in them I am grateful to the Committee of the Islamic Research Association for accepting to publish this text and translation in their admirable series.

---

[1] It should however be noted that the diacritical points are frequently omitted in the manuscript, so that in some passages the correct reading must remain a matter for conjecture.

[2] That this did happen is shown by the statement in Junayd's letter quoted in *Kitāb al-Lumaʿ*, p. 240 ; cf MS. Şehit Ali of his *Rasāʾil*, fol 4a

IN THE NAME OF GOD, THE MERCIFUL, THE COMPASSIONATE.

Praise belongs to God, and peace be upon His servants, whom He hath chosen. Thus said the Shaykh, the Imām, the Gnostic, Abū Sa'īd Aḥmad ibn 'Īsā al-Baghdādī al-Kharrāz (God sanctify his spirit and illumine his grave !) :

I said to a certain learned man [1]. "Inform me concerning Truthfulness, its nature and meaning, as well as how it may be practised, that I may be acquainted with it ".

He replied. "Truthfulness is a word embracing and entering into all meanings. Desirest thou that I shall answer thee briefly and summarily thy question, or that I should expound to thee both the theory and the practice, together with the stems from which the branches spring ? "

I said : "I desire both these things together, that it may be for me at once a theoretical knowledge, a practical science, and a help in life ".[2]

He replied. "If God wills, thou shalt be guided aright. Know first that a disciple, if he have a strong faith, and desires to walk in the way of salvation, must be acquainted with three principles, that he may practise them : for thereby his faith will be strengthened, its inward realities standing firm, and its branches being established,[3] while his acts will be pure and sincere, if God wills.

"The first of these principles is Sincerity, in accordance with God's words, 'So do thou worship God in *sincerity* of

---

[1] It seems probable that this form of dialogue, with the attribution to a spiritual instructor of the doctrine, is a mere literary fiction. the same form is frequently met with in the works of Muḥāsibī.

[2] *'Ilm* is the theory, *fiqh* its practical application.

[3] Sc. all forms of religious knowledge, of which faith is the fountain-head.

religion, for verily, God's is the *sincere* religion '.[1] God also
says, ' Then call ye on God, being *sincere* to Him in your religion '.[2]
God said to Muḥammad (God bless him and give him peace) .
' Say, Verily I am bidden to serve God, being *sincere* to Him in
religion ' [3] Again God says, ' Say, God do I worship, being
sincere in my religion to Him '.[4] God also says, ' And mention
in the Book Moses , verily he was *sincere*, and he was a messenger,
a prophet '.[5] Such sayings as these are many in the Qur'ān,
but this will suffice.

The second is Truthfulness, in accordance with God's words,
' O ye who believe, fear God, and be with those that are *truthful* '.[6]
God also says, ' If they were *true* to God, it would be better for
them '.[7] Again, God says, ' Men who have been *true* to their
covenant with God ' [8] ; and again, ' And mention in the Book
Ishmael ; verily he was *true* to his promise ' [9] ; and again, ' That
He might ask the *truthful* of their *truthfulness* ' , [10] and again,
' *Truthful* men and *truthful* women '.[11] In the Qur'ān is much
of this.

The third is Patience, in accordance with God's words,
' O ye who believe, be *patient*, and vie in *patience* '.[12] God also
says, ' And if ye are *patient*, it is better for the *patient* , (6 *a*)
be thou therefore *patient* : but thy *patience* is only in God '.[13]
Again, God says, ' And be thou *patient* in the judgment of thy
Lord, for verily thou art in our sight ' [14] ; and again, ' And be
patient with what they say, and flee from them decorously ' [15] ,
and again, ' And hold thyself *patient*, with those who call unto
their Lord morning and evening, desiring His face ' [16] , and again,
' And be ye *patient*, for God is with the *patient* ' [17] , and again,
' And give good tidings to those that are *patient* ' [18] (for God in

---

[1] Q xxxix, 2-3.   [2] Q. xl, 14.   [3] Q xxxix, 14.
[4] Q xxxix, 16.   [5] Q. xix, 52.   [6] Q ix, 120.
[7] Q. xlvii, 23.   [8] Q. xxxiii, 23.   [9] Q. xix, 55.
[10] Q xxxii, 8.   [11] Q. xxxiii, 35.   [12] Q. iii, 200.
[13] Q. xvi, 127.   [14] Q. lii, 48.   [15] Q. lxxiii, 10.
[16] Q. xviii, 27.   [17] Q. viii, 48.   [18] Q. ii, 150.

such good tidings shows His special grace to them). This is frequent and affirmed in the Qur'ān.

These three words bear various meanings, and enter into all actions : indeed, no act is complete without them, and if any act is lacking in them, that act is imperfect and incomplete Nor is any of these three principles complete without the other two, and so long as one of them is lacking, the others are void. Sincerity is not complete, save there be Truthfulness therein and Patience thereover , Patience is not complete, save there be Truthfulness therein and Sincerity therein , Truthfulness is not complete, save there be Patience thereover and Sincerity therein.

The first of all acts is Sincerity. It is also thy bounden duty to believe in God, and to know, affirm, and bear witness that there is no god save God only, Who has no partner, and that He is ' the first and the last, the outward and the inward ',[1] the creator, maker, former, provider, dispenser of life and death, unto Whom ' do things return ' [2] that Muhammad is His servant and messenger, bearing truth from the Truth ; that the prophets are true, being truly endowed with apostlehood, and excellent in counsel , and that paradise is true, and the resurrection, and the return to God, Who ' forgives whom He pleases, and punishes whom He pleases '.[3] This must be thy inward belief and spoken profession, without doubt or hesitation, thy heart being at rest and acquiescing in what thou hast averred and affirmed : so that there shall not occur to thee, in respect of all that has come from God upon the tongue of His Prophet, any doubt concerning all that he has mentioned on his Lord's behalf. Thou shalt not oppose the practice of the Prophet and his Companions, and the Imāms of right guidance, who were a model to the righteous who came after them, and the Followers, and the learned doctors of every age. Thou shalt follow in all this the community of true believers, being sincere therein to God alone, and seeking naught but God, that thy resignation and thy faith and thy belief may be perfect.

---

[1] Q lvii, 3.   [2] Q. ii, 206.   [3] Q. iii, 124 , v, 21.

1. TRUTHFULNESS IN SINCERITY.

Truthfulness in Sincerity is the second [principle], (6*b*) and it is this that God enjoins when He says, ' Then let him who hopes to meet his Lord act righteously, giving his Lord no partner in his service of Him ' [1] Now the exposition of this text is, that a man should desire God in all his acts and deeds, and his motions altogether, both outward and inward, not desiring thereby aught other than God, with his mind and knowledge standing guard over his spirit and heart, being watchful of his purpose, and seeking God in his whole affair ; and that he should not love the praise or applause of others, nor rejoice in his acts performed before his fellows. Rather, if aught of this occurs to him, he will be on his guard against it with swift revulsion, and will not acquiesce in it : and when any man applauds him, he will praise God, because He protected him, when He assisted him to do what good thing his fellows saw him engaged upon Yea, and he is at that time afraid because of the corruption of his acts, and his inward impurity that is hidden from men, but not hidden from God : and thereat he trembles, fearing lest his secret thoughts be proved fouler than his outward acts. For so it is related in the Tradition : ' When the secret thought is fouler than the outward act, that is an outrage ; and when the secret thought and the outward act are equal, that is just balance , but when the secret thought is superior to the outward act, that is pre-eminence '.[2]

It is the duty of a man, therefore, that he should keep his actions secret, so far as in him lies, that none may overlook them, save only God : so will he the sooner attain God's good pleasure, gain an ampler reward, draw nearer to salvation, be more secure against the wiles of the enemy,[3] and be further removed from faults. It is related that Sufyān al-Thawrī [4] said : ' I care not what of my actions is manifest '. It is also

---

[1] Q. xviii, 110.   [2] Non-canonical.

[3] Sc. Satan, as always in Ṣūfī writings.

[4] The famous traditionist, theologian and ascetic, died 161 h.

related in the Traditions that the secret act surpasses the public act seventy times [1]; and that a man may perform an act in secret, and Satan will leave him for twenty years, and after that invite him to display it, so that that act will be transferred from the secret to the public register, and he will be deprived of much of the reward and merit of the deed; after which Satan will continue to remind him of his deeds one by one, to the end that he may make mention of them to his fellows, and take pleasure in their witnessing them, and satisfaction in their applause, so that he becomes a hypocrite.[2] All these things are the very opposite of sincerity.

Now this which we have mentioned is merely a general summary of sincerity, which every creature must know and practise, and of which none should be ignorant. Over and beyond this remains (7a) a superlative degree of sincerity, which a man will attain, when he is once firmly established in these principles."

I said : " And then what ? "

He replied : " So much as can be mentioned thereof is this : that a man should not hope save for God, nor fear save God, nor adorn himself save unto God ; and that he should not be affected by any man's faultfinding for God's sake, nor care who is angry with him, so long as he faithfully follows the course wherein God's love is, and His good pleasure. As for what remains to be told, to wit the supreme perfection of sincerity, this is still greater : so much, however, will suffice for the instruction of disciples now treading the path.

2. TRUTHFULNESS IN PATIENCE.

Next is Truthfulness in Patience. Now patience is a word with several meanings, both outward and inward. As for its outward significations, these are three : the first is patience in performing God's ordinances in every state of life, in hardship

---

[1] Non-canonical.　　　　　　[2] Non-canonical.

or in ease, in security or in affliction, willingly or perforce ; the
second is patience in abstaining from all that God has forbidden,
and in restraining the wayward inclinations and desires of the
soul for such things as God does not approve, willingly or perforce. These two kinds of patience, which operate in their
respective fields, are a duty imposed on all men for their per-
formance. The third is patience in performing works of supererogation and pious acts, whereby a man is brought near to God,
if he constrains himself to achieve perfection therein, because of
the reward which he hopes to obtain from God. So it is related
of the Prophet that he said, among other sayings of divine
authority : ' In no way does my servant so draw near to Me
as by performing those duties which I have imposed on him ,
and my servant continues to draw near to Me through acts of
supererogation, until I love him ' [1] There is also a fourth kind
of patience, which consists in accepting the truth from any
man who imparts it to thee, and admonishes thee unto it,
accepting it because truth is a messenger from God to His
servants, which they may not reject for whoever declines to
accept the truth, and rejects it, in reality rejects God's commandment. This then is the outward aspect of patience, which
is binding on all creatures of this they may not be ignorant, for
it is indispensable to them. Over and beyond this remains
the exposition of the realities and perfection of patience, which
is the concern of those that are patient, after they have become
firmly established in the patience which we have mentioned."

I said : " What is patience in itself, and what is its manifestation in the heart ? "

He replied " Patience consists in enduring what the soul
abominates, and it is manifested when something occurs (7b)
which the soul abominates · for then the soul drinks it to the
dregs, banishing impatience, and refraining from publishing or
complaining, concealing what has come upon it It is related

---

[1] The famous *hadīth qudsī*, attributed by Massignon (*Essai*, p. 106)
to Abū Dharr.

in the Traditions : ' Whoso makes public, complains '.[1] Hast thou not heard the words of God ? ' Those who repress their rage, and those who pardon men '.[2] Seest thou not that such a man represses the thing which he abominates, and which his soul finds wearisome to endure, so that he becomes patient ? But if he displays impatience, and requites him who has done evil against him, and does not pardon him, he goes forth from the bounds of patience. This, then, is upon this analogy "

I said " Wherein does the patient man find strength to be patient, and how is his patience perfected ? "

He replied : " It is related in the Traditions that patience in enduring hateful things is of the beauty of sure faith [3] ; it is also related that patience is the half of belief, while sure faith is the whole of belief.[4] Now the reason for this is, that when a man believes in God, and has faith in God's promises and threats, there arises in his heart a yearning for the reward which God has promised, and at the same time his heart is pervaded by a fear of the punishment which God has threatened. Then is his yearning true, and firm his resolve to seek salvation from what he fears, while his expectations are aroused, that he will obtain that for which he hopes. He renews therefore his quest and his flight ; fear and hope take up lodging in his heart. Then he mounts the steed of patience, and drinks its bitterness to the dregs, when this comes upon him · he proceeds to the accomplishment of his resolves, and is fearful lest they be not fully achieved. So there falls to him the name of *patient*.

3. TRUTHFULNESS IN REPENTANCE.

Truthfulness is a word with many meanings. The first part of truthfulness is, truthfulness in turning to God in sincere repentance. God says · ' O ye who believe, turn unto God with sincere repentance '.[5] God also says . ' And turn ye all

---

[1] Non-canonical. [2] Q. iii, 128. [3] Non-canonical
[4] Non-canonical, but found in Ghazālī. [5] S. lxvi, 8.

repentant to God, O believers, that haply ye may prosper '.[1]
Again, God says : ' God has turned towards the Prophet and
those who fled with him, and the Helpers '.[2]

Now the first part of penitence is this : to regret any transgression against God's command and prohibition, and to resolve
not to revert to anything which God abominates ; ever to be
asking God's forgiveness, and to recompense every wrong done
to the property and effects of others, making confession to God
and them ; to continue in fear and sorrow, trembling (8a) lest
thou prove not thy sincerity ; to be fearful lest thy repentance
be not accepted, and not to be confident that God has not seen
thee engaged in aught He abominates, and therefore hates thee.
So al-Ḥasan al-Baṣrī [3] said : ' What shall make me confident
that He has not seen me engaged in aught He abominates,
and said, Do whatsoever thou wilt, I will not forgive ? ' It is
also related that he said : ' I am fearful lest He cast me into the
Fire, and care not '. I have heard that a certain theologian
met a man, and said to him : ' Hast thou repented ? ' The
other replied : ' Yes '. He asked : ' Hast thou been accepted ? '
The other said : ' I know not '. The first said : ' Depart, for
I know '. Another said ' The grief of the bereaved mother
passes away, but the grief of the penitent does not pass
away '.

It is further necessary, to truthfulness of repentance, that
thou shouldst give up all friends and boon-companions who have
assisted thee in setting at naught God's commandments, and
that thou flee from them, and count them for enemies, unless they
return to God. For God says : ' Friends on that day shall be
foes one to the other, save those who fear God '.[4] Truthfulness
of repentance also demands that all wickedness shall depart
from thy heart, and that thou beware of secretly yearning after
the remembrance of aught from which thou hast turned to God.

---

1 S. xxiv, 31.   2 S. ix, 118.
3 The famous ascetic and wāʿiẓ, died 110 h.
4 S. xliii, 67.

God says : ' And leave the outward part of sin, and the inward part thereof '.[1]

Know, moreover, that the more the believer is sound of heart, and increases his knowledge of God, so much the stricter his repentance ever becomes. Consider how the Prophet says : ' Verily my heart is constricted, and I ask pardon of God and turn to Him a hundred times in every day '.[2] When a man's heart is pure of sins and defilements, and is filled with an in-dwelling light, no more is it concealed from him what secret blemish enters the heart, or how it is ever hardened with the resolve to backslide, before ever any deed is done : and he repents accordingly.

4. TRUTHFULNESS IN SELF-KNOWLEDGE.

Next is truthfulness in self-knowledge and self-control. God says : ' O ye who believe, be ye steadfast in justice, wit-nessing before God though it be against yourselves, or your parents, or kinsmen '.[3] In the story of Joseph God says [through the mouth of Joseph] : ' And I do not clear myself, for the soul is very urgent to evil, save as my Lord has mercy '.[4] Again, God says : ' But as for him who feared the station of his Lord, and forbade the soul its lust, verily Paradise is the resort '.[5] The Prophet of God said : ' Thy greatest enemy of all is thy soul which is within thee, then thy people, then thy son, then thy kinsmen '.[6] (8b) It is also related that he said : ' A soul—its braying and whining shall be its protection before God to-morrow '. Someone asked : ' What is that ? ' He replied : ' Your souls which are within you '.[7]

---

[1] S. vi, 120.

[2] This well-known tradition occurs, in the commoner form (seventy for a hundred) in Muslim, _Dhikr wa-da'awāt_ 41. The _Kitāb al-ighānah_ of al-Baqlī is based on it (see Ritter in _Der Islam_ XXI, p. 103).

[3] Q iv, 134.　　　[4] Q. xii, 53.　　　[5] Q. lxxix, 40-41

[6] Non-canonical.

[7] Non-canonical : the text slightly restored.

The man who is truthful in his quest for God summons his soul to obey God, and to seek His pleasure : and if it responds to him, he praises God, and entreats it fair. So it is related of Abū Hurayrah [1] that he was seen smoothing out something which he had spread on the ground : being asked what it was, he replied, ' It is my soul ; if I do not entreat it fair, it will not support me ' If, however, such a man finds that his soul does not respond to him, to do what is pleasing to God, or if he sees that it is tardy, he denies it the things in life which it loves most, and opposes it in its desires ; he makes war upon it for God's sake, and complains of it to God, until he amends it. He does not continue to revile it, while entreating it fair, and making mention of its faults, reviling it and all its actions of which he does not approve, and yet continue with it in doing what it desires. So it is related that a certain theologian said : ' I know that part of my soul's amendment is, that I should know that it is corrupt   it is enough sin in a man, that he should be aware of a fault in his soul, and yet not amend it, nor be turned from it to repentance '. Another theologian said : ' If thou art truthful in thy self-condemnation, be not angry if another man condemns thee for aught '.

If thy soul wrestles with thee concerning any lust, or if thy heart is occupied with seeking for anything, be it unlawful to thee or lawful, do thou suspect it, as one that desires its amendment, and do thou prevent it therefrom, as one that desires its subjection. In refraining it from all pleasures, constrain it to hold fast to the example of those who have gone before.[2] It is certain that the matter concerning which it wrestles with thee is one of two things : either it is unlawful, so that it would merit the wrath [of God], or it is lawful, so that it would be compelled to stand long at the questioning [3] Those who have quitted unlawful things have done so out of awe and reverence for God ; while they withstood lawful things in a spirit of zeal and

---

[1] Traditionist : died 57 or 58 h.

[2] Sc the " leaders " mentioned in the next paragraph.

[3] Viz. on the Day of Judgment.

emulation. Work therefore to wean thyself from both states : for if a man weans himself from this world, he shall be suckled by the world to come ; and if he takes the world to come for his mother, he will desire to be filial towards it and to visit it, for so the children of this world are satisfied to take it for their mother, being filial towards it and labouring after it.

Cast away from thy heart those that prefer this world, and dismiss them with friendly counsel (9a) and warning. Beware lest thou lag behind the leaders. Consider this carefully in the privacy of thy own soul, and thereunto urge thy friends and companions. For the leaders girded their loins and bound up their skirts, baring their heads and shanks they revelled in their fitness, and competed one with the other in eager haste, respecting God's right, lest they rend any veil which He had forbidden them, and showing their love for Him by rejecting even that which He had permitted them to take. They forewent the unlawful thing in a spirit of service, but the lawful thing they eschewed to draw near to God. They were familiar with vigils and thirsting, being content with little competence, and expecting small recompense

5. Truthfulness in Knowledge of the Devil

Next is truthfulness in the knowledge of thy enemy, the Devil God says : ' Verily, Satan is to you a foe, so take him for a foe · he only calls his crew to be inmates of the blaze '.[1] Again, God says . ' O sons of Adam, let not Satan tempt you, as he drove your parents forth from Paradise ' [2] He also says : ' For Satan had made seemly to them their works, and turned them from the path '.[3]

'Abdullāh ibn Mas'ūd [4] said ' The angel has one sort of enticement, and Satan another . the angel entices with the promise of something good, Satan with the promise of something

---

[1] Q xxxv, 6.   [2] Q. vii, 26   [3] Q. xxvii, 24.

[4] Famous traditionist : died 32 or 33 h. The two sayings which follow are of course traditions.

evil '. In another narration he says : ' Satan is brooding over the heart of man : when he recollects God, he shrinks away, but when he is forgetful, he whispers '.

Cut off his supplies, by being resolved to oppose thy lust, and to restrain thy soul from transgression and reaching out, for these twain are his allies against thee, and by them his guile is reinforced But if thou followest them, then summon thy intellect and the knowledge which God has taught thee, and with these stand watchful over thy soul, guarding thy heart and all that enters into it   If there be aught of goodness and knowledge, follow after it . but if it be of falsehood and evil desire, then with all speed banish it.   Tarry not overlong with any dangerous thought, lest the thought become a lust, and the lust an urge, and the urge an act.

Know that thy enemy, the Devil, is not unmindful of thee, whether in silence or speech, prayer or fasting, giving or withholding, journeying or home-dwelling, solitude or company, steadiness or dispatch, gazing or averting the gaze, slothfulness or energy, laughter or weeping, concealing or advertising, (9b) grief or joy, health or sickness, questioning or making answer, knowledge or ignorance, farness or nearness, movement or repose, penitence or obstinacy He spares no pains to weaken thy resolve, to enfeeble thy purpose, and to put off thy repentance.   He postpones thy pious intention again and again, but commands thee to expedite what it would not harm thee to put off, desiring thereby to cut thee off from good.   Then, in the instant when thou art engaged in works of piety and obedience, he reminds thee of things thou needest, to sever thee from any good in which thou art engaged.   Sometimes he makes it seem desirable to thee to migrate from one land to another, making thee suppose that the other land is better than that in which thou art, to occupy thy heart, and deprive thee of any settled place, causing thee to do what thou wilt afterwards regret doing.

Do thou then be most cautious of thy enemy, and fortify thyself against him by taking refuge with God, Who is the

surest stronghold and the strongest support : so make God thy
cave and place of refuge. Beware of thy enemy when thou art
angry or irascible : if the recollection of God comes upon thee,
at the time when thy anger is aroused, and thou knowest that
He is watching thee, at once, fearing Him, thou wilt extinguish
the fire of indignation and the blaze of fury, being afraid lest
He Who sees thee, as thou knowest, should rightly be angered
at aught thou committest in thy anger. Satan takes advantage
of thee when thy anger is aroused, or thy desire vehement. As
for bewaring of him when thou art irascible, it is said that Satan
says : ' We never despair of the irascible man, though by his
invocation he bring the dead to life , for an hour will come
upon him when he is passionate. and we will do with him whatever
we wish '. ' But whoso takes tight hold on God, he is guided
unto a right way '.[1]

6. TRUTHFULNESS IN GODLINESS.

Next is Truthfulness in Godliness, and the right use of
piety. Truthfulness in godliness consists in departing from every
doubtful thing, and quitting every matter which appears dubious
to thee So it is related that the Prophet said : ' No man is
truly pious, until he leaves alone that in which no harm is,
for fear of that in which there is harm '.[2] He also said :
' Manifest are lawful things, and manifest unlawful things, and
between them are the doubtful matters '.[3] (10a) Whosoever
quits doubtful things, for fear of falling into what is unlawful,
has wholly purified himself. Ibn Sīrīn [4] said : ' Nothing is
easier in my religion than godliness : I quitted everything that
appeared dubious to me '. Al-Fuḍayl [5] said : ' Men say that
godliness is difficult. [But I say,] leave that which causes thee

---

[1] Q. iii 96. [2] Non-canonical.
[3] For this tradition see Bukẖārī, *Imān* ch. 39 ; Muslim, *Mubāḥāt*
107, 108, etc.
[4] Died 110 h. [5] Ibn ʿIyāḍ : d. 187 h.

to doubt, for the sake of that which causes thee no doubt [1] ;
take only what is lawful and good, and from what is lawful do
thy utmost to seek only the thing that is pure, for God says:
O ye apostles, eat of the good things, and do right ' [2] The Prophet
said to Sa'd · ' If thou desirest that God shall answer thy prayer,
eat what is lawful '.[3] 'Ā'ishah said : ' O messenger of God,
who is the believer ? ' He replied ' The man who in the
evening considers whence his bread has come '.[4]

7   Truthfulness concerning what is Lawful

Next is Truthfulness concerning what is Lawful and Pure,
its nature and enjoyment. Truthfulness concerning what is
lawful is this . having ascertained a thing to be lawful, to take
thereof only so much as is necessary, according to thy knowledge
of thyself, and of what excites thy evil inclinations. Cast not
on thy soul any burden above its strength, lest it be broken ;
follow it not to its extravagant desires ; take as much as will
sustain thee, avoiding meanness as well as extravagance, in
what concerns food, dress and shelter. Beware of vain trifles,
as thou fearest the reckoning and the long waiting. It is related
that a certain man said to 'Alī ibn Abī Ṭālib : ' O father of
Ḥasan, describe to us this present world '. He said : ' What is
lawful thereof is a reckoning, and what is unlawful is a punishment (or, a recompense) '.[5] When a man is weak, and some
good thing comes into his possession, he keeps it to himself, and
to any whom he is sustaining : if he expends any of it on charity,
he does so fearing the while that, once it has left his possession,
he will not be able to endure [its loss] with patience, and so will
fall into an even worse state. Yet, while he keeps it to himself,
he despises himself for hoarding it, because his soul has no

---

[1] A tradition : cf. Bārizī, *Taysīr al-wuṣūl* IV, p. 31.
[2] Q. xxiii, 53.   [3] Non-canonical   [4] Non-canonical.
[5] This probably represents a variant in the form the narrative
follows.

trust in God, and will not rely on Him instead of that thing. So he continues, until his purpose becomes stronger."

I said "How is it that the prophets had possessions and lands, such as David, Solomon, Abraham, Job, and the like ? How is it that Joseph was over the treasures of the earth,[1] (10b) and Muhammad, and the righteous men after him ? "

He replied : "This is an important question, involving a big issue   Know that the prophets, and the learned and pious men who came after them, were the trustees of God's secret in His earth, and of His commandment, prohibition, and know-ledge · they were His depositaries, and for His sake counselled those whom He created and made   For they understood God's commandment and prohibition, and comprehended why He created them, what He desired of them, and to what He called them , they were agreeable to His desire, and entered into every matter according to His will   So they stood in the station of intelligent servants, accepting [the word] of God, and preserving His testament.   They hearkened unto Him with the ears of their understandings attentive, and their hearts pure, and fell not short of His calling , for they heard God saying . ' Believe in God and His Apostle, and expend of that wherein He hath made you to be successors ' [2]   God also says . ' Then made We you their successors in the earth after them, that We may see how ye will act '.[3] Again, God says . ' To God belongs what is in the heavens and what is in the earth '.[4] God further says : ' Surely His is the creation and the bidding '.[5]   So these men were certain that they and their souls belonged to God, and likewise that all which He bestowed on them and gave them to possess was His ; save that they were in an abode of trial and affliction, and were created for trial and affliction in this abode.

So it is related of 'Umar ibn al-Khaṭṭāb that when he heard the words, ' Has there come upon man a portion of time when he was not a thing remembered ? ',[6] he said : ' Would that it

---

[1] Cf. Q. xii, 55.   [2] Q. lvii, 7.   [3] Q. x, 15.
[4] Q. ii, 284.   [5] Q vii, 52.   [6] Q. lxxvi, 1.

were finished ! ' ([bý this] 'Umar meant before the recitation of
' verily, we created man from a mingled clot, to try him ').[1]
Then he muttered (in the commentary this word, *hamham*, is
explained as meaning, he had a certain disability in recitation).
'Umar, then, by saying ' Would that it were finished ! ' meant,
would that he had not been created when he heard God saying,
' when he was not a thing remembered '. This was because
'Umar knew what God's rights involved, and the power of His
command and prohibition, man's inability to fulfil them, and
God's just claim against him in respect of his shortcomings, as
well as what God has threatened to do with man in punishment
for his transgressions.

It is likewise related that al-Hasan [2] said . ' God only caused
Adam to descend into this world as a punishment, and appointed
it to be his prison, when He expelled him from His neighbour-
hood, and transferred him to the abode of toil and trial '.   In
the Traditions it is said · ' When God created Adam, before
breathing into him His spirit, He, knowing what would come
(11a) of his seed, desired to destroy him ' [3]   (Abū Sa'īd says :
A distinguished and noble man has said, ' Would that he had
indeed destroyed him, so that he had not been created ! ').[4]

As for the man who works for God, and is truthful, when he
possesses aught in this world, he firmly believes that that thing
belongs to God, not to himself, except in so far as it may involve
a duty, God having bestowed it upon him to try him, until he
has discharged the duty.   For a blessing is a trial, until man
discharges his duty of gratitude therefor, using it as help towards
obedience to God : in like manner misfortune and hardship are
a trial and an affliction, until a man is patient thereunder, and
so discharges his duty to God.   On this matter a certain philosopher has said : ' All theory is an affliction, until it is practised '.   God says : ' Who created death and life, to try you ' [5] ;

---

[1] Q. lxxvi, 2.   [2] Presumably al-Baṣrī.   [3] Non-canonical.
[4] An insertion into the narrative by the author.
[5] Q. lxvii, 2.

and again : ' And We will surely try you, until We know which of you strive strenuously, and which are patient, and test the reports concerning you '.[1]

The prophets, and the pious men who came after them, being made aware by God that He afflicted them in this world by means of plenty and the bestowing of possessions, put their trust in God, and not in their possessions : they were God's treasurers in respect of what He gave them to possess, spending it in fulfilment of their duties to God, without shortcoming or transgression or faintness. They assigned no contrary interpretation to God's purpose, and took no pleasure in their possessions · their hearts were not concerned with what they possessed, nor did they exclude other men from its enjoyment.

So it is related of Solomon, son of David, and the possessions and special favours which God allowed him, when God says : ' This is Our gift, so bestow thou of it or withhold, not being called to account .[2] The commentators explain . ' not being called to account in the world to come, for it was a mean gift, a sign of favour from God to him '. The learned have related that Solomon used to feed his guests on whitened flour, and his children on unsifted corn, while he himself ate barley-meal. They also relate that Abraham never ate save with a guest. Sometimes no guest would come to him for three days together, and he would fast ; and sometimes he would walk a parasang, less or more, to search out a guest   (11b) Likewise, whenever the prophet Job heard any man taking God's name in vain, he would return to his house, and make expiation for him.   The learned also relate that, although Joseph was over the treasures of the earth, yet he never ate his fill.   Being asked concerning this, he said . ' I fear to take my fill, lest I forget what it is to hunger '.   It is further related of Solomon, that one day the wind was supporting him, and the birds drew near to him, while Jinns and men were with him.   Now he had on him a new

---

[1] Q. xlvii, 33.   [2] Q. xxxviii, 38.

2

shirt, and the garment clung to his body, and he felt pleasure thereat : and at once the wind was stilled, and set him down upon the earth. He said to the wind · 'What ails thee ? ' The wind replied : ' We were only commanded to obey thee so long as thou wast obedient to God '. So he considered within himself wherein [his disobedience] had occurred : and he remembered, and repented, and the wind forthwith supported him [again]. It is reported that the wind used every day to set him down several times for like cause

These men, therefore, whilst yet in the midst of their possessions, were in reality without them. They took delight in the recollection and service of God, and did not content themselves with their possessions, nor losing them found aught amiss. In nothing took they joy, so that they needed no cure or effort to expel such things from them. God said to His Prophet : ' These are they whom God hath guided, so by their guidance be thou led ' [1]

Now it was to this same Prophet that Gabriel appeared, at the time when Gabriel was transformed [2] ; and behold, an angel came down from heaven, who had never come down before Gabriel said : ' I feared that it was he who had come down with a command for me '. He came to the Prophet with a greeting from God, and said to him : ' These are the keys of the treasures of the earth, that they may be thine, both gold and silver · in them thou mayst dwell until the Day of Resurrection, and they shall in no wise lessen the portion that is laid up for thee with God '. But this the Prophet did not choose, but said : ' Once I hunger, and once I am filled ',[3] counting this to be an affliction and a trial from God. He did not reckon this to be a matter left by God to his free-will, for if it had been so he would have accepted it. He knew that the love of God consists in

---

[1] Q vi, 90.

[2] So into the shape of a man. The incident is that described by the commentators on Q. liii, 9.

[3] Non-canonical.

quitting this world, and turning from its gaudy splendours, for in this God had schooled him, when He said : (12a) ' And do not strain thine eye after the good things wherewith we have provided a few of them—the gauds of the present life, to try them thereby '.[1] It is also related that one day he put on a mantle with a badge, and then cast it from him, saying . ' Its badges almost distracted me (or, its badges distracted me)[2] : take it, and bring me an Anbijānī cloak '.[3] It is likewise related that a gold seal-ring was made for him, wherewith to seal his letters to whatever person God commanded him to admonish ; he put it on, and then cast it from his hand, saying to his companions ' One glance at it, and one glance at you '.[4] It is further related that on one occasion he changed the strap of his shoe, and put a new one in its place ; then he said · ' Give me back the first strap '.[5]

So every heart that is pure and undefiled yearns after the next world, and knows that God is watching over him : he therefore fears greatly lest he should secretly repose in the possession of this world, and take delight in aught that is of it. Such stories are common in the tales [of the saints].   The intelligent, quick-witted man needs but a hint to this

When Muhammad urged his Companions to almsgiving, Abū Bakr brought all his possessions (and he was the most powerful of the people) ; and the Prophet said to him   ' What hast thou left for thy children ? ' ' God and His Prophet ', he replied, ' and with God I have an increase '   Note, then, that Abū Bakr reposed in God, not in any material thing   possessions had no value in his sight, for he took more pleasure in what was laid up with God. Seeing where his duty lay, he left

---

[1] Q xx, 131   [2] Recording a variant in the tradition.

[3] For this tradition see Ibn al-Athīr, *Nihāyah* I, p. 46, Yāqūt, *Mu'jam al-buldān* VIII, p 168 f.

[4] Cf. Bukhārī, *Libās* ch 46, 55 , Muslim, *Libās* 54, 55 ; Ibn Sa'd, I/II, p. 165 f.

[5] Non-canonical.

nothing at all, saying : ' I have left God and His Prophet '.
Then came 'Umar with half his possessions. The Prophet said :
' What hast thou left for thy children ? '   ' Half of my possessions ', he replied, ' and with me God has an increase '. So
he gave one half of his possessions, saying, ' and with me God has
[an increase] '. Lastly came 'Uthmān, ready to equip the " army
of difficulty " [1] entirely, with all it had need of, and to dig the
well of Rūmah.[2]

Note, then, that these men reckoned the material possession
as belonging entirely to God.   As for our statement, that these
men were " without " their possessions, whilst they were still
in their hands, counting them as God's, (12b) this is proved by
the saying attributed to the Prophet   ' We are the company of
prophets ; we do not bequeath, and what we leave behind is for
alms '.[3] Note that during their lifetime they grudged God
nothing · likewise they bequeathed nothing, but left it all to
God, even as it was God's whilst it was in their hands ; they
neither added to it, nor bestowed it upon any man that came
after them.   Surely this is eloquent to the man who understands
about God, and does what is just

Such was the case with the Leaders of Guidance after [the
death of] God's Prophet.   When Abū Bakr succeeded to the
leadership, and the world in its entirety came to him in abase-
ment, he did not lift up his head on that account, or make
any pretensions.   He wore a single garment, which he used
to pin together, so that he was known as the " man of the
two pins ".   'Umar ibn al-Khaṭṭāb, who also ruled the world
in its entirety, lived on bread and olive-oil.   His clothes were
patched in a dozen places, some of the patches being of

---

[1] The expedition against Tabūk in 9 h.   For ' Uthmān's generosity
on this occasion, cf. the authorities cited by Wensinck, *Handbook*, p. 240 :
add Ibn Hishām, p. 895.

[2] Cf. Ibn Hishām, p. 673.   For Abū Bakr giving all, see Wensinck,
op. cit., p. 7 ; for ' Umar giving half, *ibid.*, p. 235.

[3] Bukhārī, *Khums* ch. 1, *I'tiṣām* ch. 5.

leather , and yet there were opened unto him the treasures of Chosroes and Caesar. As for 'Uthmān, he was like one of his slaves in dress and appearance Of him it is related that he was seen coming out of one of his gardens with a faggot of firewood on his shoulders. When questioned on the matter, he said : ' I wanted to see whether my soul would refuse '. Note, then, that he was not heedless of his soul, and of [the necessity of] making covenant with it and training it. When 'Alī succeeded to the rule, he bought a waist-band for four dirhams, and a shirt for five dirhams ; finding the sleeve of the garment somewhat long, he went to a cobbler, and taking his knife cut off the sleeve level with the tips of his fingers · yet this same man divided the world right and left. When al-Zubayr died, he left behind him debts amounting to more than two hundred thousand [dinars], all contracted through liberality and extravagant generosity. Talḥah ibn 'Ubaydillāh gave away all his possessions, even to his family jewels, to beggars.

All this proves that these men were truly as God described them, when He said · ' And expend of that whereof He has made you successors '.[1] Yet not one man of the people (13a) of our time is ashamed of this, for all that he possesses doubtful things : but God knows well what manner of things they are, and whence they came, what value they have in the man's heart, and how he prefers them and reposes in them instead of in God, as well as his innumerable sins in busying himself and occupying himself therewith. One of them has even asserted [2] that he has possessions in precisely the same manner as those who lived before him, and adduced them as an excuse for following the dictates of his own evil desire, despite the fact that his life is totally at variance with the practice of these people. Nay, but to confess one's shortcomings to God, as being a neglectful servant, and to ask God to advance him to the same high station as that these men attained, this is nearer to salvation. God is [our] help.

---

[1] Q. lvii, 7.
[2] This same argument is answered by al-Muḥāsibī, Naṣā'iḥ, ch. 3.

8. Truthfulness in Abstinence.

Next is Truthfulness in Abstinence, its nature and practice.
Now God has abused the present world, naming it with names
such as none ever before bestowed on it. He says . ' The life of
this world is but a sport, and a play, and a gaud, something to
boast about amongst yourselves '.[1] Shall not he be ashamed,
who understands of God, that God may see him taking satisfaction in what is a play and a sport, in this abode of deception ? "

I said . " What is the true nature of this world ? "

He replied · " Men of insight and wisdom are agreed that
" this world " means in reality the soul and its desires This is
proved by God's words : ' Made seemly unto men is the love of
lusts for women, children, hoarded talents of gold and silver,
horses of mark, cattle, tilth—that is the enjoyment of the life
of this world ' [2] All these things which God mentions are of the
soul's desire and delight, and by them the soul is distracted
from the recollection of the world to come ; and when a man
quits what his soul desires, he quits this present world. For
consider well, it is possible for a man to be poor and without
possessions, and yet to covet this world, and to desire the fruits
thereof, resolving that if only he could obtain what he desires of
it, he would take it for his enjoyment and have pleasure therein.
Such a man is reckoned by God among the lustful, according to
the degree of his ambition, only his portion at the reckoning
is less than theirs who have attained it and had enjoyment of it.

The first degree of abstinence is abstinence as to following
the desires of the soul. When a man finds his soul amenable, then
he no more cares in what state he may be, night or day . for
therein he is conformable with God's desire, (13b) for that he
opposes his soul, and prevents it from attaining its desire of
lusts, pleasures. recreations, the company of friends and boon-
companions, men heedless of God—save only such as have been
disappointed of the very thing which he himself desires . for

---

[1] Q. lvii, 19.   [2] Q. iii, 12.

truly it is a fault in a man to keep company with those who desire what he desires. Next, he takes only the bare necessities of food, drink, clothing, shelter, sleep, speech, talking, listening. He foregoes all longing for things of this world, and bewares of finding it agreeable ; for the Prophet himself has said : ' This world is delicate and fresh '.[1] That man therefore pictures this world to himself as passing away, and foreshortens his hopes of it : he lives in expectation of death, and longs for the next world, yearning to make his lodging in that everlasting abode. To this end he labours, putting all ease from his heart in ceaseless reflection, and from his body in ceaseless service. This, then, is the first degree of abstinence.

Sufyān al-Thawrī,[2] Waqī' ibn al-Jarrāh,[3] Ahmad ibn Hanbal,[4] and others have said that abstinence in this world is the foreshortening of hopes, and this proves what the philosophers have said , for when a man restricts his hopes, he takes no pleasure, and so heedlessness is far removed from him. A certain sect have said : ' The man who is abstinent in this world yearns after the world to come : he has set it up before his eyes, so that it is as if he sees the punishment and reward which are in it, and therefore he turns away from this world '. So it is related that the Prophet said to Hārithah [5] · ' How farest thou this day, O Hārithah ? ' He replied . ' Believing truly, O messenger of God '. ' And what ', asked the Prophet, ' is the truth of thy belief ? ' The other answered : ' I have turned my soul away from this world. Therefore I have thirsted by day, and watched by night, and it is as though I behold the Throne of my Lord coming forth, and the people of Paradise taking joy together, and the people of Hell making moan together '. Then the Prophet said : ' A believer whose heart God has illumined. Thou hast known, so hold fast '.

---

[1] Tirmidhī, *Fitan* ch. 26.   [2] Died 161 h.

[3] Died 197 h.   [4] Died 241 h

[5] Died 2 h. This story is a favourite with the Ṣūfīs, cf. Kalābādhī, *al-Ta'arruf*, p. 73, 78, etc.

A certain theologian has said : ' Abstinence is when the value of things has departed from thy heart '. Now abstinence in the matters of this world is a very delicate and hidden subject : every man (14a) has his own form of abstinence, according to the degree in which he knows God. If a man banishes from his heart the desire for this world little by little, so that he may see whither his abstinence is leading him, or if he is feeble in dealing with himself, and will not oppose his soul's desires, he has never turned from this world, and does not yearn after the world to come. A certain theologian has said : ' The man who is truly abstinent in this world neither blames the world nor praises it, neither rejoices in it when it comes to him nor grieves for it when it turns from him '."

(Abū Sa'īd al-Kharrāz says, A certain distinguished man has said : ' No man is completely abstinent, until gold and stone are equal in his sight : and gold and stone are not equal, until he has a sign from God, so that the stone is changed into gold, and thereby the value of things departs from his heart '. I heard the same man also say : ' Stone and gold were not equal in the sight of any of the Companions after [the death of] the Messenger of God, with the exception of Abū Bakr ')

I said : " To what end have the abstinent been abstinent ? "

He replied : " To divers ends Some were abstinent in order to free their hearts of every occupation, making all their purposes one, namely, to obey God in recollection and service ; and in this God sufficed them. So it is related that the Prophet said ' Whoso makes his purpose a single purpose, him God will suffice for all his purposes '.[1] Jesus said : ' Verily I say unto you, the love of this world is the head of every sin, and in possessions is a great sickness ' They said : ' O Spirit of God, what is its cure ? ' He answered : ' That a man shall not be paid his due '. They said : ' And if he is paid his due ? ' He replied. ' There will be pride and vanity in him '. They said :

---

[1] Ibn Mājā, ch. 2.

' And if there is no pride or vanity in him ? ' He answered : ' His desire to amend will distract him from the recollection of God '.

Others were abstinent in order to lighten their backs, that they might swiftly pass over the way,[1] when the heavy-burdened are held back for questioning. So it is related that the Prophet said · ' My companions came to me, and I noticed that 'Abdurrahmān ibn 'Awf was not among them (or else he said, He was detained from me) [2] · so I said, What has delayed thee in coming to me ? He replied, I was engaged in counting over the quantity of the increase of my riches, until so much sweat streamed from me that if there had come (14b) to drink of it seventy camels, thirsty from eating *hamḍ*,[3] they would have gone away satisfied '.[4] It is also related on several authorities that the Prophet said · ' Those who are greater shall be less on the Day of Resurrection, save only those who have poured out their wealth thus and thus, to left and right, among God's servants '.[5] He also said : ' No man is there, be he rich or poor, who will not wish on the Day of Resurrection that God had made his sustenance in this world only his daily bread ' [6] Abū Dharr [7] relates that the Prophet said . ' It would not please me that I should have gold as much as [the mountain of] Uhud to spend in God's path, and that a third of the night should pass over me, while I still had more than one dinar of it, kept in case of a debt ' [8]

Others were abstinent out of a desire and longing for Paradise, and this consoled them for the loss of this world and its pleasures, until they yearned long after the reward unto

---

[1] Sc. of A'rāf, on the last day.

[2] Recording a variant.   [3] A bitter herb.

[4] For his wealth, see Ibn Sa'd III/I, pp. 92 ff.

[5] Bukhārī, *Istiqrād* ch 3, *Riqāq* ch. 14 ; Muslim, *Zakāh* tr. 32.

[6] Cf. Ibn Mājā, *Zuhd* ch. 9   [7] Died 32 or 33 h.

[8] Bukhārī, *Riqāq* ch. 14 , Muslim, *Zakāh* tr. 31, 32 ; Ibn Mājā, *Zuhd* ch. 8.

which God had called them, and which He had described to them. In the Traditions it is related that God says : 'As for those who are abstinent in this world, unto them I grant Paradise '.[1] A certain theologian has said : ' No recitation is good without abstinence '.

The highest degree of abstinence in this world was attained by those who conformed with God's wishes. These were men who understood of God : they were intelligent and loving, and they listened to God's condemnation of this world, and how He has belittled its worth, and does not approve of it as an abode for His saints. They were ashamed that God should see them inclining towards anything which He has condemned and not approved. This they imposed upon themselves as a duty, for which they sought no recompense from God. They nobly conformed with God's wishes, and God ' wastes not the hire '[2] of him who does good. For those who conform with God in all their affairs are the most intelligent of His servants, and enjoy the highest price with God. So it is related that Abū 'l-Dardā'[3] said · ' How sweet is the sleep of the intelligent, and how sweet their breakfasting ! How they have despoiled the vigils and fastings of fools ! An atom's weight of the man of piety and sure faith weighs more with God than mountains' worth of the deeds of those who are deceived '. Surely this is eloquent to the man who understands (15a) of God God is [our] help.

It is related that 'Umar ibn 'Abdil-'Azīz once saw a youth who was pale, and said to him . ' Whence comes this paleness, boy ? ' The youth replied · ' From sicknesses and distempers, O Commander of the Faithful '. ' Tell me truly ', said 'Umar. ' Sicknesses and distempers ' said the youth. 'Umar said : ' Tell me how '. The youth replied · ' O Commander of the Faithful, I have turned away my soul from this world, and its stone and gold are become equal in my sight , and it is as if I behold the people of Paradise in Paradise visiting each other, and the people

---

[1] Non-canonical.   [2] Cf. Q ix, 121, etc.   [3] Died 31 h.

of Hell in Hell making moan together'. 'Umar said : 'How comes this, boy ? ' The youth said : ' Fear God, and He will pour forth knowledge copiously upon thee. Verily, when we were foreshortened of the knowledge of what we practised, we gave up practising even that which we knew · but if we had practised in accordance with what knowledge we had, we should have inherited a knowledge which our bodies could not have supported ' [1]

It is related that Abū Bakr al-Ṣiddīq once asked for a drink. He was brought a vessel : but when he had put it to his mouth and tasted it, he thrust it aside, and wept. On being asked about this, he said : ' I saw the Prophet of God one day, pushing away with his hands, as though something were falling, and yet I saw nothing. So I said to him, O messenger of God, I see thee pushing away with thy hands, and yet I see nothing. He said, Yes · this present world appeared before me, in all its gauds ; and I said, Get thee from me ! But it answered, Thou shalt not escape from me, nor shall any escape from me that comes after thee. (Abū Bakr continued) So I fear that it has overtaken me '. Now there was in the vessel from which he drank water and honey . and yet he wept, being afraid of that.

It is related in a Tradition that the Companions of Muḥammad neither ate to have pleasure, nor dressed to take delight. Another version says that when Muhammad's Companions grew in worldly power, after his death, and the whole world lay conquered at their feet, they wept because of it, and were afraid, saying : ' We fear, lest our good deeds have been rewarded in advance '.[2] Wherefore let a man fear God, and be just, and let him cleave to the path of those who have gone before, acknowledging his shortcomings, and asking God to support his stumblings.

---

[1] After the Tradition, ' If a man acts according to what he knows, God will teach him what he knows not '.

[2] Sc. in this world, instead of in Paradise.

9.' TRUTHFULNESS IN TRUSTING.

Next is Truthfulness in Trusting to God.   (15b) God says :
' Let the believers therefore trust ' [1] ; and again, ' And in God
do ye trust, if ye be believers ' [2]; and again, ' Verily God loves
those who do trust '.[3]   It is related that the Prophet said :
' There shall enter Paradise of my community seventy thousand
without reckoning · these are they that neither make auguries,
nor brand themselves, nor use spells, but trust in their Lord '.[4]
'Umar ibn al-Khaṭṭāb relates that the Prophet said ' If ye
trusted in God as ye should, He would sustain you even as He
sustains the birds, which in the morning go forth hungry, and
return in the evening filled ' [5] 'Abdullāh ibn Mas'ūd [6] said
' Power and wealth go about seeking after trust : when they
have found it, they abide [in it] '.

Now Trust in itself, and its manifestation in the heart, is
this : to believe in God and to rely on Him, taking rest and
assurance in Him as regards all that He has guaranteed , to
expel from the heart all anxiety over the affairs of this world,
and the means of sustenance, and every matter of which God
Himself has taken charge ; and to know that of every matter of
which man stands in need, be it of this world or the next, God
is the ruler and provider, for none but God can bring it to him,
and none but God can withhold it from him   In trust, all desire
and trepidation must depart from the heart, with all fear, if
these be connected with other than God : for a man must have
confidence in Him, and a full knowledge and firm conviction
that God's hand is outstretched towards him, to provide him
with all that he seeks ; for no good thing shall befal him, save
by God's command, nor any evil thing overtake him, save with
His leave.   So it is related that al-Fuḍayl said . ' The man who

---

[1] Q. iii, 118, etc.   [2] Q. v, 26   [3] Q iii, 153.
[4] Bukhārī, Ṭibb ch. 17, 42; Riqāq ch. 21, 50. Muslim, Imān tr.
372, 374 ; Tirmidhī, Qiyāmah ch. 16.
[5] Ahmad ibn Ḥanbal, I, pp. 30, 52.   [6] Died 32 or 33 h.

trusts in God, and has confidence in Him, has no suspicion of Him, and does not fear that He will desert him '.

So, when a man trusts in God, and God gives him to possess anything of this world, and aught thereof remains over with him, he does not lay it up for the morrow, save with the intention that the thing belongs to God, and is in trust for God's rights, and that he is a treasurer of God : then, when he sees a fitting occasion, he quickly brings it forth, and expends it on succouring [others] ; for in all that he possesses, he and his brethren have equal rights. This is binding upon him in the first instance only in respect of members of his household, and near relatives, and men of piety, and then in respect of the whole community of Muslims whenever he sees them to be in a state of dire need, (16a) he changes their deficient circumstances.

It is related that the Prophet said : ' Abstinence in this world does not consist in making unlawful what is lawful, or in wasting wealth : true abstinence in this world is this, that thou shouldst have greater reliance in what is in God's hands than in what is in thy hands, and that, when any misfortune befals thee, thou shouldst rejoice more in the reward which it brings thee, than if it had been removed from thee '.[1] Bilāl[2] said : ' I once came to the Prophet with a date, and he said to me, What is this ? I said, Something which I have stored up for thy breakfast. He said, Spend, Bilāl, and fear not that He Who sits upon the Throne will suffer thee to want. Didst thou not fear that this will reek in Gehenna ? '[3] 'Ā'ishah is reported to have said : ' I am not like Asmā' (meaning her sister) ; Asmā' takes nothing for the morrow, but I collect one thing for another ' It is also related that one day she was raising her arm and scattering dirhams, when her maidservant said to her : ' Wilt thou not leave one dirham for some meat ? ' She replied : ' Why didst thou not remind me ? ' 'Ā'ishah relates that on the night of the Prophet's last illness he appeared all the while

---

[1] Non-canonical.   [2] Died 20 h.   [3] Non-canonical.

to be terrified, and in the morning he said : ' What has that *dhuhaybah* [1] done [with me] ? ' (Now its value was fifty-six dirhams.) Then he said · ' Bring it forth : for what would be Muhammad's thoughts, if he met his Lord with that in his possession ? ' [2] Masrūq [3] is reported to have said . ' I am never more confident in God than when my servant-girl says that we have nothing in the house '."

I said " Does trust in God exist along with secondary causes, or by severing connection with secondary causes ? "

He replied . " By severing the greater part of secondary causes : for then one passes direct to the Causer, and rests in Him."

I said · " Does the trustful man undertake any cure or medical treatment ? "

He replied . " This matter has three different aspects. A certain sect of men God has chosen, to have nothing to do with either cures or secondary causes, for the Prophet said   ' There shall enter Paradise of my community seventy thousand men without a reckoning   these are they that neither brand themselves, nor use spells, but trust in their Lord '   The Prophet also said . ' He does not trust, who brands himself and uses spells '.[4] Again, he said   (16*b*) ' If a man is turned back by an evil omen, he has associated himself with unbelief ' [5] Nevertheless, the Prophet commanded the use of drugs and spells, and the making of incantations, and even ordered that Ubayy ibn Ka'b's [6] vein should be cut , but this is explained by al-Mughayrah ibn Sha'bah [7] thus . ' Of the seventy thousand whom the Prophet specially chose, those who branded themselves and used spells were not trusting '. Some theologians have interpreted the matter in the same fashion. Apart from this, everything that is lawful to other men was lawful also to them, and

---

[1] A small piece of gold   [2] Cf. Ibn Sa'd, II/II, p. 32 f.
[3] Died 10 h.   [4] Ahmad ibn Hanbal, IV, pp. 251, 253.
[5] Cf. Ahmad ibn Hanbal, II, p 220.
[6] Died 22 h.   [7] Died 50 h.

in no way vitiated their trust in God : for they possessed both intellectual and spiritual knowledge, and their eyes were turned to the Lord of sickness and cure, Who at His will either harms or profits by the cure. For many a man has sought to be cured by a remedy which has proved to be [an augmentation of] his sickness, and many a man has died of his remedy, or of the cutting of a vein. Many a man has sought to be healed, and has hoped to be helped by the very thing which has proved his undoing, or has feared to be harmed by the very thing which has saved him. The truthful man, who confides and trusts in his Lord, does so because he knows that He is sufficient for him, above all that He has created · he does not miss anything which God has withheld from him, because God ' is sufficient for him, and He attains His purpose '.[1]

I said : " What of the man who says, I trust in God that I may be defended [from evil] ? "

He replied : " This saying must mean one of two things. Either he means that God will defend him from all that causes impatience and fretfulness through the gift of trust, without any change in the course of events as destined by God this is our view, and the view of those who believe in predestination. Or else he means that God will defend him from whatever he may pray to be defended against, no matter what it may be, as with the man who said, ' Wild beasts will not devour me because of my trust in God, and whatever comes to me of my own seeking will also come to me without seeking ; for trust protects me against everything that causes me to fear, if I pray to God to defend me ' ; a saying which need not astonish us, for sometimes the man who trusts in God is defended, and sometimes he is not, and yet his trust is in no way impaired."

I said · " How is this ? Explain this to me somewhat."

He replied : " Very well. When John the son of Zachariah was slaughtered by a cruel woman on a charger, he did not trust

---

[1] Q. iii, 65.

in God [1] , and when Zachariah was sawn asunder with a saw,
he did not trust in God ; and so with all the prophets who were
slain, or made to endure suffering . (17a) and yet they were of
all men the most powerful in faith, and the most truthful.   So
Muhammad, when he fled to the cave with Abū Bakr, and they
hid there [2] , and when the polytheists broke his tooth, and dabbled
his face with blood [3] : he did not trust in God   For consider,
true trust consists in leaning upon God, and resting in Him,
and then in submitting to His command, for ' He does whatsoever He wills ' [4]

'Abdullāh ibn Mas'ūd is reported to have said that God's
words, ' And whosoever trusts in God, He is sufficient for him,
verily God will attain His purpose ',[5] mean, He is fulfilling His
purpose ; while ' God hath set for every thing a measure ' means,
a term, a limit which the man reaches · the trustful man would
not say, *My* need will be fulfilled   This interpretation of Ibn
Mas'ūd implies, that the man who trusts in God seeks refuge
in Him knowing that the matter will not be accomplished, save
on the part of God, Who by His own power gives and withholds.
The man who trusts in God takes it not amiss when aught is
withheld, and by his trust does not seek to extort a gift : for
greed does not determine whether a thing is given or withheld,
but it is God Who both withholds and gives   Sometimes a man
is given a thing because of his trust, and sometimes the thing is
withheld in spite of his trust.   It may happen that one will see
the Magian, the infidel, the atheist, the sinner, the waster, the
liar, the unbeliever, the mocker, all disbelieving, and yet having
their needs fulfilled, while the trustful man, who is filled with
truth and firm belief, will not have a single need fulfilled, so
that he dies in misery and contempt.

---

[1] Sc. to the point of expecting that God would change what He had
decreed.

[2] On the occasion of the hijra.

[3] At the battle of Uhud, see Ibn Hishām, p. 571.

[4] Q. iii, 35.   [5] Q. lxv, 3.

Trust, then, consists in giving up being satisfied with the material things of this world, and in banishing both the appetite for and the despair of created beings : the trustful man knows that he is moving towards what is known [in God's foreknowledge], and he is well-pleased with God, being aware that he cannot through trust obtain the hastening of what God has postponed, or the postponement of what God has hastened. He has succeeded in expelling impatience and trepidation, and has found rest from the torment of covetousness : having trained his soul in knowledge both intellectual and spiritual, he says, ' What is destined will be, and what will be is surely coming '. So a certain philosopher has said · ' Take revenge on thy covetousness through contentment, even as thou takest revenge on thy enemy through retribution '. One of the Companions said : (17b) ' I entered the house of the Prophet, and there was in the house a dried date ; and the Prophet said, Take it : if thou hadst not come to it, it would have come to thee '.[1] Muḥammad ibn Ya'qūb[2] relates that he was told by Aḥmad ibn Ḥanbal, who had it on the authority of al-Mu'allī[3] via Marwān ibn Mu'āwiyah,[4] that Anas ibn Mālik[5] said : ' The Prophet was given a number of birds as a present. He gave a bird to a maid-servant to eat, and on the morrow she brought it to him. He said, Have I not forbidden thee to lay up provision for the morrow ? '[6]

It is indispensable for every man to know this much about trusting . but the supreme perfection of trusting is mightier than this.

10. TRUTHFULNESS IN FEAR.

Next is Truthfulness in the Fear of God God says : ' Me therefore dread . . . and Me do ye fear '.[7] Again, God says : ' And fear not men, but fear Me '[8] ; and again, ' They fear their Lord above them '[9] ; and again, ' So none fears God of

---

[1] Non-canonical.   [2] Died 270 h.
[3] Probably ibn Manṣūr al-Rāzī, died 211 or 212 h.
[4] Died 193 h.   [5] Died 93 h.   [6] Uncanonical.
[7] Q. ii, 38.   [8] Q. v, 48.   [9] Q. xvi, 52.

3

His servants save. those that know ' [1] , and again, ' Nor shall
ye do a work, save that We be witness over you, when ye are
engaged therein ' [2] , and again, ' He knows what is in your souls,
so beware of Him '. [3]　The Prophet said to Ibn 'Abbās [4] :
' Fear God, as though thou seest Him '. [5]

Now as for what stirs up fear, until it lodges in the heart,
this it is : to be continually in awe of God, both secretly and
openly, knowing that God sees thee, and that none of thy
motions, be they outward or inward, is concealed from Him.
Then He has a high place with thee in all thy motions, both
inward and outward, so that thou art cautious lest He see in thy
heart aught that He likes not and does not approve, and keepest
watch over thy intention, since He knows what is in thy soul.
If a man keeps it firmly fixed in his heart, during all his motions,
that God sees him, and then, with God's help, turns from whatever displeases God, his heart will be pure and illumined, and
fear will lodge therein.　He will continually beware of God, and
in all his states he will be afraid.　God's commandment will
take a large place in his heart : through God he will not be
affected by the reproach of any man, and for God's sake every
man who sets at nought God's commandment will be small in
his sight.

The account of fear is long these are its principles, which
if a man uses them will bring him to the realities [of fear].　This
is the outward aspect of fear : over and beyond this remains the
greater part of its quality.　(18a)

11.　TRUTHFULNESS IN SHAME.

Next is Truthfulness in the Shame of God.　It is related
that the Prophet said : ' Shame is of faith '. [6]　He is also reported

---

[1] Q. xxxv, 25.　　　　[2] Q x, 62.　　　　[3] Q ii, 236

[4] Died 68, 69 or 70 h.

[5] Bukhārī, *Imān* ch 37 ; Muslim, *Imān* tr. 1, 5, 7.

[6] Bukhārī, *Imān* ch. 3, 16 ; Muslim, *Imān* tr. 57-59 ; Aḥmad ibn
Ḥanbal, II, p. 9, 56.

to have said : ' Shame is entirely good '.[1] He further said :
' Be ye truly ashamed of God. Whoso is truly ashamed of God,
let him guard his head and what it contains, his belly and what
it holds, and let him remember the grave and the affliction
[therein]. Whoso desires the next world, quits the gauds of this
world '.[2] Again, the Prophet said : ' Be ashamed of God, as
thou wouldst be of an upright man among thy own people '.[3]
A man said : ' O messenger of God, what shall we show of our
secret parts, and what conceal ? ' He replied : ' Veil thy secret
parts, save from thy family and that which thy right hand
possesses '. The man said : ' Suppose one is alone ? '[4] The
Prophet answered : ' It is more proper to be ashamed of God '.[5]
Whenever Abū Bakr went to a privy, he used to cover his head,
saying . ' I am ashamed of my Lord '. All these sayings prove
how near God was to these men for if a man is ashamed of
God, he sees God watching over him and witnessing him in every
state."

I said · " What is it that stirs up shame ? "

He replied . " Three characteristics [first], God's kindness
towards thee, and thy failure to be grateful, whilst continuing
in misconduct and transgression , secondly, the knowledge that
thou wilt be in God's sight in thy place of returning and lodging [6] ;
and thirdly, the recollection that thou wilt stand before God,
and that He will question thee about things, both great and
small "

I said : " And what fortifies and strengthens shame ? "

He replied : " The fear of God, when the wayward desire
enters into the heart, so that the heart is frightened and scared :
for it knows that God sees what is in it, and therefore the shame

---

1 Non-canonical.

2 Non-canonical, but quoted by Qushayrī, Risālah, p 128.

3 Non-canonical.

4 In the privy.

5 Abū Dāwud, Hammām tr 9 ; Tirmidhī, Adab ch 22, 39.

6 Sc. the grave.

of God is established   If it continues in this, the shame will increase and wax strong ."

I said : " And what is it that begets shame ? "

He replied : " Apprehension lest God should turn from one in hatred, being displeased with what one has done."

I said : " What prevails in the heart of one who is ashamed of his Lord ? "

He replied : " Fear for the vision of Him Who sees him : for then he is afraid of God, and therefore ashamed of Him." (18b.)

(Abū Saʿīd says   I heard a disciple ask a gnostic, " What is the sign of the awe of God in the heart of him who knows God ? " The gnostic replied : " When adder and fly are equal in his sight.")

I said : " How is shame weakened ? "

He replied : " By giving up self-examination and godliness."

I said : " What are the inward states of him who is ashamed ? "

He replied . " Persistent humility, continual lowliness, bowing the head, restraining the glance, gazing little at the sky, blunting the tongue so that it does not speak overmuch, being afraid to uncover in a privy, giving up frivolity and laughter, and being ashamed to enter upon even that which God has allowed, not to mention any accidental thing which God has forbidden.

Men differ from each other in the degree of shame, according as God is near to them and they to Him.

12. TRUTHFULNESS IN THE KNOWLEDGE OF GOD'S BENEFITS AND IN GRATITUDE TO HIM

Next is Truthfulness in the knowledge of God's benefits, and in gratitude to Him. God says : ' But We have been gracious to the sons of Adam, and We have borne them by land and sea, and provided them with good things, and preferred

them above many that We have created '.[1] Again, God says :
' And if ye would number the favours of God, ye cannot count
them '[2] God also says . ' Remember my favours wherewith
I have favoured you '.[3]

When a man awakes from heedlessness, he considers and
beholds God's blessings towards him, how they have been perfected both of old and now. As for His former blessings, these
are . that He remembered thee before thou wast anything at
all, and privileged thee with a belief in His unity, faith in Him,
and the knowledge of Him ; He also caused the Pen to inscribe
thy name on the Preserved Tablet as a Muslim. Then He
caused the intervening ages to pass away, and set thee in a
company of believers who have found salvation, bringing thee
forth into the best of communities and the noblest of religions,
of which same community is His friend Muḥammad. Then He
guided thee unto the traditional faith, and dealt with thee in the
religious law, keeping thee far from errors and heresies. Then He
brought thee up, and protected thee, and fed thee, until the ordinances [of Islam] became binding on thee.[4] Yet thou didst forget
His blessing, neglecting to preserve His testament, and for a space
of thy life indulging in evil desire : but in all this He exacts no
recompense for thy sinning, but rather veils thee, and is clement
towards thee, looking upon thee. Then He inclined towards
thee (19a) after all this, when thou hadst been refractory, and
He wakened thee out of thy heedlessness, teaching thee how
thou hadst failed in obedience ; and He granted thee conversion
unto Him, and settled thee in His good pleasure. Now therefore there remains for thee, as thy bounden duty, gratitude
upon gratitude : which of His blessings canst thou number,
and for which of them be grateful ? Yet must thou know and
practise gratitude.

Gratitude is of three kinds : gratitude of the heart, of the
tongue, and of the body. Gratitude of the heart is, to know

---

[1] Q. xvii. 72   [2] Q. xvi, 18.   [3] Q. ii, 38.
[4] Sc. at the age of attaining manhood.

that all blessings come from God alone, not from any other ; gratitude of the tongue is, to praise and laud Him, publishing His benefits and making mention of His kindness ; gratitude of the body is, not to use any member, which God made sound and fair of form, in any act of disobedience, but to obey God therewith.   Likewise, thou wilt make all the things of this world, which He has given into thy hands to possess them, an aid for thyself in obeying Him, not converting them to vanity, nor spending them in extravagance.   Finally, thou wilt pay service unto God, and accord Him all thy effort.   So it is related that the Prophet one day stood until his feet became swollen.   They said to him : ' O messenger of God, what is this toil ?   Has not God excused thee ? '   He replied   ' Shall I not be a grateful servant ? ' [1]

God says . ' Work, O family of David, thankfully '.[2]   Again, God says : ' If ye are grateful, I will surely give you increase '.[3] When a man attains to the perfection of gratitude to God, he pauses, and considers, and lo, his very gratitude is a blessing from God, requiring that he should be grateful to God therefor, since He has set him among those that are grateful.   Thereafter he labours in the gratitude of gratitude ; and he is wellnigh bewildered, so swiftly kindness follows kindness, from God to him, with goodness and all manner of graces.

We are told that Moses prayed to his Lord thus : ' O Lord, Thou hast commanded me to be grateful for Thy blessing, and my very gratitude is a blessing from Thee '   Then God revealed to him : ' Thou hast truly attained knowledge, since thou knowest that that is from Me, and thou hast thanked Me '. 'Umar ibn 'Abdil-'Azīz said : ' To recollect a blessing is itself an act of gratitude, and blessings indicate (19b) the love of Him Who blesses '.

---

[1] Bukhārī, *Tafsīr* on S. xlix, ch. 2.

[2] Q. xxxiv, 12.

[3] Q. xiv, 7.

13. TRUTHFULNESS IN LOVE.

Next is Truthfulness in Love. Now the philosophers are
agreed that love springs from the recollection of blessings. Ibn
'Abbās relates that the Prophet said . ' Love God because of the
blessings wherewith He nourishes you ; love me because of
[your] love of God , and love the people of my house because of
[your] love of me '.[1] God says : ' And those who believe are
stronger in love for God '.[2] I have heard that God made revela-
tion to Jesus, saying : ' O Jesus, verily I say unto thee, I am
more loving to My servant who believeth than his soul which is
within him '. We are told that al-Ḥasan al-Baṣrī said : ' Men
said, in the time of God's messenger, O messenger of God,
verily we love God with a strong love. Then God appointed a
sign for His love, revealing : If ye love God, follow me, and
God will love you '.[3]

It belongs to truthfulness in love to follow the Prophet in
his conduct, abstinence, and character, taking him for an example
in every matter, and to turn from this world and its gaudy
beauty : for God made Muḥammad to be a sign and a guide,
a proof to His community. It also belongs to truthfulness in
the love of God to prefer God's love in every matter above thy
soul and thy desire, and in all thy affairs to begin by doing His
commandment before that of thy soul. We are told that Moses
said : ' O Lord, make testament to me '. God said : ' I make
Myself testament to thee '. Moses said · ' O Lord, how makest
Thou Thyself testament to me ? ' God said : ' If two matters
come to thee, one being from Me and the other from thyself,
then thou shalt prefer the love of Me above thy desire '.

He that loves God, lays it upon himself as a duty to recollect
God with both heart and tongue · he frees himself from heedlessness, and seeks pardon therefor ; and so all his members are
but a legacy in trust, to serve Him Who loves him. He neither
forgets nor neglects : his whole purpose is to please Him Who

---

[1] Non-canonical.   [2] Q. ii, 160.   [3] Q. iii, 29.

loves him, and he labours with all his might to be conformable with Him, performing His ordinances, and eschewing what He has forbidden. He adorns himself before God in all his strength, fearing lest there come (20*a*) upon him any matter which shall cause him to fall from the sight of Him Who loves him. So it is related, on more than one authority, that the Prophet said : ' God says, My servant draws not so nigh Me, as by performing what I have ordained for him to do · but through works of supererogation he continues to draw nigh unto Me, until I love him ; and when I love him, I am for him both hearing and sight, hand and helper. He calls Me, and I answer him : he counsels Me, and I counsel him '.[1] The mark of love is, to be in accord with the Beloved, in every matter to walk with Him along His paths, to draw near to Him by every means, and on His course to flee from every matter which does not help him therein."

I said : " Is love according to the number of blessings ? "

He replied : " The beginning of love is the recollection of blessings : then it proceeds according to the capacity of the recipient, that is, according to his deserts. For the true lover of God loves God both when receiving His blessings, and when His blessings are withheld · in every state he loves Him with a true love, whether He withholds or grants, afflicts or spares him. Love invariable attaches to his heart, according to his compact [with God] : except that it is nearer to superfluity.[2] For if love went according to the number of blessings received, it would diminish when the blessings diminish, in times of hardship and when affliction befals. But he is God's lover whose mind is distraught for his Lord, and who is only concerned to please Him when he is grateful to God, and when he recollects Him, he is bewildered, as though no blessing ever descended on any man, but that it descended on him also. His love for God

---

[1] See p. 6, n. 1.

[2] It is better to love more than to love less.

distracts him from all [concern with] creation. The love of God has banished from his heart all pride, rancour, envy, iniquity, and much that concerns his advantage in the affairs of this world—and how much more the recollection of what concerns him not !

A certain philosopher has said : ' If a man is given somewhat of love, and is not given a like degree of fear, he is deceived '. It is related that al-Fuḍayl ibn 'Iyāḍ said : ' Love is more excellent than fear '. Ismā'īl ibn Muhammad [1] relates that he heard Zuhayr al-Baṣrī [2] say : ' I met Sha'wānah,[3] and she said to me, How excellent is thy path, except that thou deniest love. I said, Do I deny it ? She said, Lovest thou thy Lord ? I said, Yes. She said, Then how fearest thou that He may not love thee, seeing that thou lovest Him ? I said, I love him because of the knowledge and the blessings which He has abundantly showered on me (20a) but I have sinned, and I fear that He may not love me because of what I have done. Thereupon she fainted : and when she recovered, she said, Fie ! ' (Abū Sa'īd says : How excellently this man spoke ! This is a true saying.)

(Abū Sa'īd says · A certain exalted and distinguished man has said, " The man who loves God is of great moment, compared with the man whom God loves ".)

God is [our] help. This is eloquent to those whom God has helped and directed · but over and beyond this remain greater qualities of lovers.

14. TRUTHFULNESS IN ACQUIESCENCE.

Next is Truthfulness in Acquiescence with God. God says : ' Nay, by thy Lord ! They will not believe, until they have made thee judge of that whereon they differ ; then they will not

---

[1] Perhaps al-Zuhrī, died 134 h.

[2] Probably ibn ' Abdillāh, see Ibn Ḥajar, *Tahdhīb al-tahdhīb* III, p. 346 f.

[3] See Sha'rānī, *al-Tabaqāt al-kubrā* I, p. 78.

find within themselves aught to hinder what thou hast decreed, and they will truly submit '.[1] A certain theologian has said : ' God did not attest their faith, as long as they did not acquiesce in His Prophet's decree : how much less, if they had not acquiesced in His own decree ! ' "

I said : " What is the sign of acquiescence in the heart, and what is its manifestation ? "

He replied : " It is the heart's joy in the course of destiny. A certain man has said . ' Acquiescence is meeting calamities with hope and cheerfulness '. It is related that Anas ibn Mālik said : ' I was a servant of the Prophet. He never said to me, with regard to any matter, Why didst thou do that ? or, Why didst thou not do that ? He would only say, So it was destined, and so it was decreed '.[2] 'Umar ibn al-Khaṭṭāb is stated to have said : ' I care not how I find myself at night or morning, whether it be in a state agreeable or disagreeable to me, for I know not which of the twain is better for me '. 'Umar also said : ' If I had patience and gratitude for camels, I would not care which of them I rode '. This saying of 'Umar is an indication of acquiescence, because one is patient only with regard to something disagreeable, and grateful only with regard to something agreeable ; and he said, ' I care not which of the twain has fallen to my lot ' · this was because the two states were equal in his sight.

It is related that 'Abdullāh ibn Mas'ūd said : ' How delightful are disagreeable things ! By God's oaths, they are naught other than riches and poverty · each has its attendant duty—of riches, philanthropy, and of poverty, patience ' (21a) 'Umar ibn 'Abdil-'Azīz said ' Today I am without choice in any matter '. A certain man said : ' And I have no blessings, save the workings of destiny in me, whatever may befal '. This same man drank poison. When they said to him, ' Take an antidote ', he replied : ' If I knew that my cure could be accomplished by touching my nose or my ear, I would not do it '. The Prophet said to

---

[1] Q. iv, 68.   [2] Non-canonical.

Ibn Mas'ūd : ' O son of a slave's mother ! Be not overanxious . whatever is destined will be, and whatever thou art given for sustenance thou wilt eat '.[1] The Prophet said to Ibn 'Abbās (the story is a long one) : ' So if thou canst work for God with acquiescence, in sure faith, it is well : if not, then in enduring patiently what thou hatest is great good '[2] Note that the Prophet called him to the higher of the two states. A certain philosopher has said : ' When a man has achieved perfect abstinence, trust, love, faith and shame, then his acquiescence is true '. This is our view also : otherwise, acquiescence may manifest in men at different times and on different occasions, according to the degree of their faith, and from it they return to patience. A certain man has said · ' Acquiescence is a small thing The believer's succour is patience '."

I said " Expound to me the saying of the philosopher, ' The acquiescent man meets calamities with cheerfulness and gladness '." [3]

He replied . " When a man is truthful in his love, there springs up between him and God a partnership of surrender. Suspicions depart from his heart, and he is content with the excellent choice of Him Whom he loves : he abides in His excellent dispensation, and tastes the food of existing through Him His heart is filled with joy, bliss and gladness, and this prevails over the pain of calamities and hateful affliction. The name of affliction becomes as it were a lock to him, from which he seeks to emerge when great troubles come upon him · for sometimes he takes delight in his realization, namely, that God sees him in his affliction, and sometimes he realizes that God has recollected him, and therefore afflicted him, because He was not heedless of him, for all His omnipotence, undertaking to amend his affairs. For it may be that God sees him complaining unto Him, as a lover complains to his beloved ; or else he laments to

---

[1] Non-canonical.   [2] Non-canonical.

[3] Cf. above, ' acquiescence is meeting calamities with hope and cheerfulness '.

God ; or else he yearns that God may see him acquiescing in Him. So says (21b) God : ' O thou soul at rest, return unto thy Lord, well pleased and well pleased with '.[1] Intelligent men hasten to acquiesce with God in this world, before they pass into the next, and therefore depart from acquiescence to acquiescence. In this sense God says : ' God is well pleased with them, and they are well pleased with Him · He has made ready for them gardens '.[2]

We have mentioned some of·the outward qualities of the acquiescent man, so much as it was possible to mention in a book but over and beyond these remain greater qualities. God is [our] help.

15   TRUTHFULNESS IN LONGING.

Next is Truthfulness in Longing after God   It is related that the Prophet used to say in his prayers : ' I ask of Thee, O God, the enjoyment of the life after death, of gazing on Thy face, and longing to meet Thee '[3]   It is related that Abū'l-Dardā' used to say . ' I desire death, longing for my Lord '. It is related that Hudhayfah[4] said : ' At death a friend comes in need . if a man regrets, he shall not prosper '. Shahr ibn Hūshab[5] is stated to have said . ' Mu'ādh[6] was afflicted with ulcers in his throat, and he said, Strangle me, if Thou wilt, for, by Thy might, I truly love Thee '.

'Alī ibn Sahl al-Madā'inī[7] used to arise, when [men's] eyes were reposing in sleep, and call out in an anguished voice : ' O Thou, from the thought of Whom the hearts of His creation are distracted by the consideration of the regret which will come upon them when they meet Him ! O Thou, from the longing

---

[1] Q lxxxix, 27-28.   [2] Q. ix, 101.

[3] Nasā'ī, Sahw ch 62.   [4] Died 36 h.

[5] Died 100 h

[6] Ibn al-Hārith, one of the ahl al-suffah.

[7] So emended . probably the same traditionist as is mentioned by al-Khatib, Ta'rīkh Baghdād XI, p. 429 ; Ibn Hajar, op. cit., VII, p. 330.

for Whom the hearts of His servants are unmindful, though His hands were outstretched towards them before ever they knew Him ! ' Then he would weep, until his neighbours wept because of his weeping. Then he would cry out . ' Would that I knew, my Master, how long Thou wilt imprison me ! Raise me up, my Master, unto Thy fair promise : for Thou knowest what violent longing hath stirred me, and how long I have waited for Thee '. Then he would fall fainting, and continue so until he stirred to perform the morning prayer.

Al-Ḥāriṯẖ ibn 'Umayr [1] used to say every morning : ' I have come to a new day, and my heart and soul are intent on loving Thee, my Master, and yearn to meet Thee . hasten then that meeting, before the black night cometh upon me '. In the evening he said the like : and so he continued for sixty years. (22a).

The man who longs after God is disgusted with this world, and with remaining therein : he desires death, and the ending of his span and lot. It is peculiar to him, that he seeks to be estranged from created things, and keeps himself alone in solitude and isolation : his occupation is with trepidation, yearning, grief, distress, sorrow , with the violence of his love his breast is choked, and blushing and incoherence overcome him when the Beloved's name is mentioned, in Whom he rejoices , his thoughts are pure, his zeal is quickened, and joy stirs in his bowels as he seeks to meet [Him]. Astonishment comes upon him, surprise, and bewilderment, at the very thought of attaining his expectation of the Expected One, so that he utterly forgets all his portion in this world and the next, except the vision of Him for Whom he longs. Yes, then at that time he is confronted with a fear that is indeed fear—that he will not attain his Beloved, but may be cut off from Him, and barred from reaching Him, and veiled from Him. Then he fears lest any accident befal him, while he is yet in the abode of affliction : long seem the

---

[1] al-Baṣrī, see Ibn Hajar, *op. cit.*, II, p. 153.

days and nights to him, until he shall depart from this world whole, and in a manner pleasing to his Lord.

These are some of the qualities of those who long [after God], so much as can be mentioned · but over and beyond these remains the greater part of their description. God is [our] help

16. TRUTHFULNESS IN INTIMACY

Lastly comes Truthfulness in Intimacy with God, and with His recollection and nearness. A certain philosopher has said : ' Intimacy with God is finer and sweeter than longing · for if a man longs, there is a slight interval between him and God by reason of his longing, whereas the intimate is nearer to God '. So it is related that Gabriel came to the Prophet in the form of a man, and questioned him concerning resignation and faith, and then concerning good works. The Prophet said to him : ' Thou shalt worship God as though thou seest Him : for even if thou seest Him not, yet He sees thee '. Gabriel replied : ' Thou hast spoken truly '.[1] It is also related that the Prophet said to Ibn 'Umar ' Worship God as though thou seest Him, for even if Thou seest Him not, yet He sees thee '. (22b) In this he indicates God's nearness, and that He is overwatching him : and from God's nearness emerge in every state the true realities of things If a man's station is fear, then through God's nearness he is affected with trepidation, terror, and fright, for he knows that He sees him ; but if his station is love, then through the realities of God's nearness he is affected with joy, pleasure, and delight, for he knows that He sees him ; he therefore hastens to seek His pleasure and proximity, so that He may see him panting with eagerness, desiring to be near to Him, and to love Him exceedingly.

If a man is patient, then, at the time of his affliction and calamity, when he is made to endure for his Master's sake things which will bring his reward nearer to him, he hearkens to the

---

[1] See p. 18, n. 2.

words of God : ' Truly God is with those that are patient ',[1]
and ' But wait thou patiently for the judgment of thy Lord,
for thou art in Our sight '.[2]   Then it is easy for him to practise
patience, and to shoulder his burden.   In like manner the people
of every station worship God in nearness, for they have certain
faith : these are they who scarcely arrive and scarcely return.[3]
As for the common people, they act only according to what they
know of God's commands and prohibitions : their hope is weak,
and they are confused, and have no certain realization.

An example of truthfulness in intimacy is afforded by the
story of 'Urwah ibn al-Zubayr [4] He asked 'Abdullāh ibn 'Umar
to give him his daughter's hand, while the latter was circum-
ambulating the Holy House of God.   Ibn 'Umar did not answer
him, or give him any reply.   After this 'Abdullāh meeting him
said to him : ' Thou spakest to me during the procession, but we
were imagining that God was before our eyes '.   With the
intimate it is as though he beholds that for which the longer
longs.

It is said that 'Abdul-Wāḥid ibn Zayd al-Baṣrī [5] said to
Abū 'Āṣim the Syrian : ' Dost thou not long for God ? '   The
other replied . ' No.   A man only longs for one who is absent :
when the absent one is present, for whom shall he long ? '
'Abdul-Wāḥid said : ' His longing is ended '.   It is related that
Dāwud al-Ṭā'ī,[6] one of the Muslim leaders, (23a) concerning
whose veracity and uprightness there is no doubt, also said :
' A man only longs for one who is absent '.   A theologian has
said : ' They only said this because of the reality of their
experience of God's nearness · it is as though they were with
Him, for they had with them an attestation which was never
absent, and this, coming from God, brought them peace and

---

[1] Q. ii, 148.   [2] Q. lii, 48.

[3] Sc. all acts of personal initiative cease.

[4] Died between 91 and 97 h.   For the story which follows see
Kalābādhī, al-Ta'arruf, p. ﻉﺀ

[5] Died 177 h.   [6] Died 162 h.

quiet, and it was a mercy and a repose accorded to them aforetime in this world [1] by God If it was not this, then what was it that they received of God through His nearness ? '

The mark of the man who is intimate with God and God's nearness is, that he experiences in his heart God's recollection and His nearness to him, and does not lose this experience at any time or in any place, whatever his spiritual state may be : God and His nearness come to him before all else. This latter occurs, when the light of God's nearness lodges in his heart : in that light he regards all things, and through that light he is guided to all things. So it is related that 'Āmir ibn 'Abdillāh [2] said : ' I have never looked at a single thing, without God being nearer to me than it '.

These two are the qualities of the intimate that he is disgusted with people and mankind [generally], and finds delight in solitude and loneliness. Being in a darkened house, he abhors a light when he sees one. he closes his door, and draws his curtain, and is alone with his heart. He grows familiar with his Lord's nearness, and becomes intimate with Him, taking delight in secret converse with Him he frees himself from any visitation which might come upon him and spoil his solitude. Yes, then one may see him dismayed even by the shining of the sun, when it enters upon him at his prayers : grievous to him is the company of other men, for they weary him , to sit with them and meet them is for him a grief and a loss. But when night covers him, and all eyes are sleeping, when every movement is stilled, and the senses of all things are quiet, then he is alone with his sorrow, and his disquietude is stirred · his sighs mount swiftly up, and long he moans, demanding the fulfilment of what his Expectation promised him, and the benefits and loving-kindnesses whereby He has aforetime sustained him. Then he obtains some part of his request, and a portion of his wants is satisfied. (23b).

---

[1] Sc. before departing to the next world.
[2] If the same as al-Jarrāh, died 18 h. See Ibn Ḥajar, *op. cit* , V, p. 73.

Moreover, the intimate feels no dismay in places where other men are afraid : alike to him are habitation, wilderness, desolation, society, and loneliness. This is because of the overwhelming sense of God's nearness which comes upon him, and the sweetness of His recollection : these prevail over all other impacts, whether outward or inward.

This is the outward aspect of intimacy, so much as can be mentioned · over and beyond this remain stations of intimacy greater and mightier than may be set down in a book, except that some hint of it may pass in conversation with those who have experienced it. God is [our] help.

Epilogue.

Know, O thou that askest concerning Truthfulness and its exposition, that this which I have mentioned to thee is only the outward aspect of Truthfulness, Patience, and Sincerity. This much it is necessary for all men to know and practise, especially disciples who seek to tread the path of salvation. Some there are who have nothing before God but this outward theory and practice · in this they labour, and in this they are truthful, and this brings them indeed to God's mercy and reward, and with God they have much good.

One man is truthful in these stations which we have mentioned, and more : this will bring him in this fleeting world to a high station, and a knowledge of God, and a noble station, so that he will pass on to joy, ease, and bliss in the gnosis of God, having attained nearness to God, and reached a noble rank too fine to be described and expounded. A certain man who knew God said . ' God bestows on His friends a grace which [His] servants cannot comprehend, either in this world or in the world to come '. Hast thou not heard the words of God ? ' No soul knoweth what delight is kept secret for them '.[1] In the Traditions we are told : ' They shall be given what eye hath

---

[1] Q. xxxii, 17.

not seen, and ear hath not heard, neither hath it entered into the
heart of man '. So it shall be with every man according to
his deserts.

Another man has unending grace in the reward of God, and
bliss in Paradise. Another has unending grace in God Himself,
(24a) and an increase of His goodness and regard. It is a true
story of the Prophet, that he said ' Of the people of Paradise
he is least in rank, who looks about his kingdom two thousand
years, to see it from end to end '.[1] Another man looks upon
the face of God twice in every day.

Now it is absurd [to say] that all these are equal, or that
their knowledge of God in this world was equal. God says .
' And We did prefer some of the prophets over others '.[2]
Superiority among men accords only with superiority in their
knowledge and gnosis of God : according to their degree in these
men differ from one another in this world and the next. God is
[our] help "

I said . " Does a man attain a state in which he no longer
seeks to attain truthfulness, in which there falls from him the
burden of religious works, the weight of sincerity, and the
burden of patience, so that he acts truthfully, and partakes in
the things which thou hast mentioned, and more, without toil
or weariness ? "[3]

He replied : " Yes. Hast thou not heard the Tradition
which relates that ' Paradise is set about with unpleasant [duties],
and Hell with evil desires ' ?[4] It is also related in another
story ' Truth is heavy but wholesome, falsehood is light but
noxious '.[5] Now the carnal soul is attached to the love of this
present abode, and is satisfied with it, loving plenty and ease
therein · but truth, and the following and practice of truth,
truthfulness, and all its characteristics—all these are opposed

---

[1] Non-canonical : cf Wensinck, *op. cit* , p. 181.   [2] Q. xvii, 57.

[3] Cf Qushayrī, *Risālah*, p. 187, where a similar question is put to
and answered by Kharrāz.

[4] Cf. Wensinck, *op. cit.*, p. 182.   [5] A well-known proverb.

to the soul's desire   When a man understands about God, and
comprehends what God has called him unto, namely, to turn
from this perishing abode, and to yearn after the everlasting
abode, then he constrains his soul to bear unpleasant things, and
to enter upon the path of truthfulness   he resolves to labour
with all his might, and is patient towards God , he toils with
his soul, and prays to God for help, and God beholds him desirous
of what is with Him, and eager to please Him   So God turns
to him, with lovingkindness and help, making easy for him what
is hard, and what he finds difficult in himself · God gives him
sweetness in exchange for bitterness, lightness for heaviness,
smoothness and ease for roughness. (24b) His nightly vigils
become easy for him , his private converse with God, and solitude
in His service, are a joy to him after his bitter struggling.
Fasting and thirsting through the heat of the day become a
light thing to him, now that he has tasted the sweetness of that
for which he hoped—God's ease and good reward.   In this way
his characteristics and states change and become easy for him,
and out of every station which he endures and suffers for God's
sake, seeking His favour, he gets a like recompense of good
So his character changes and his nature is transformed, his
carnal soul grows quiet and his intellect revives : the light of
truth lodges in him, and he grows familiar with it , evil desire
flees from him, and its darkness is extinguished.   Then it is
that truthfulness and its characteristics become part of his
nature   nothing but this finds he good, and with this only he
associates, for he is content with naught else   Then he is clothed
with his Lord's protection   then the strategy of his enemy loses
its power, and is overthrown, for his false incitements perish,
and all his armour, when evil desire dies, and the carnal soul
is fettered, so that it puts on the character of those on whom
God has had mercy   God says, in the story of Joseph . ' For
the soul is very urgent to evil, save as my Lord has mercy '.[1]
The souls of the prophets and true believers were under God's

---

[1] Q xii, 53.

mercy and protection, and so is every believer, according to the power of his faith.

Then it is that there ceases in him that labouring after truthfulness, together with the burden of practising it : for now he practises the truthfulness which we have mentioned, and many times greater than this, without trouble—nay, this becomes a delight and a nourishment to him, so that if he leaves it, he is distressed at leaving it, and feels dismayed at losing it Then truthfulness and its characteristics become an attribute of his, and no other finds he fair, until it is as though he had never been otherwise

Now the confirmation of this is to be found in the Book and the Prophetic Practice. God says . ' But those who labour for Us, We will surely guide them in our paths, and verily God is with the righteous doers ' [1] Again, God says · ' God promises those of you who believe and do right (25a) that he will give them the succession in the earth, as he did with those before them, and He will surely establish for them their religion which He has approved for them, and will give them in exchange, after their fear, security : they shall worship Me, and shall associate naught with Me '.[2] God also says : ' And We desire to be gracious with those who were weakened in the earth, and to make them leaders, and to make them heirs, and to establish for them in the earth '.[3] God says further : ' And we appointed among them leaders to guide at our bidding, for that they were patient ' [4] in the loss of this world.

We only desired to prove that a man must strive with his soul, and labour his utmost to be truthful ; and that after this, help comes from God. The proof of this is to be found in the Prophet's own practices. Ibn 'Abbās, in his commentary on the Sūrah Ṭaha,[5] says : ' The meaning of Ṭaha, in the Abyssinian

---

[1] Q. xxix, 69.   [2] Q. xxiv, 54.   [3] Q. xxviii, 4–5

[4] Q. xxxii, 24

[5] Q. xx, 1. In the commentary ascribed to Ibn 'Abbās (ed. Bombay, 1885, p. 242) this interpretation of the word Taha is given, but there it is explained as a dialect-form of Mecca.

language, is, O man. We have not sent down to thee the Qur'ān that thou shouldst be wretched—that is, in order that thou shouldst be troubled with it '. For consider, when the Prophet stood in thanksgiving until his feet became swollen,[1] he was giving thanks to God, and God commanded him to repose. It is also related that the Prophet used to worship in the mountain of Hirā' for a month or more [2] and so it is told that he used to be carefully on his guard against his enemy,[3] until this verse was revealed : ' And God will protect thee from men '.[4] Then he gave up being on the watch, for he believed God's words when He told him that He would protect him : and he had sure faith, and was quiet. In like manner with all believers, faith comes to them after weakness.

So it was that the Prophet went out to the cave in the mountain called Thawr,[5] and hid himself, he and Abū Bakr al-Ṣiddīq, and then they departed to Medina, fleeing secretly · this was only a time of trial by God, for he was in the station of patience and endeavour. Then, after he had come to Medina, the Quraysh made a raid against him, on the day of the Battle of Uhud, and slew his Companions, and broke his tooth, and dabbled his face with blood.[6] Note, then, that evil desire (25b) and labour clave to him and pursued him, as with all believers. Then, after this, he went forth, he and his Companions, crying joyfully as they drove the sacrificial beasts before them, intending to come to God's house [7] but the Quraysh prevented him from entering Mecca, so that his men were thrown into confusion, and they halted in the place which is called al-Ḥudaybiyah, and then returned, and did not enter the Sacred Territory. Now contrast this with the time when the period of

---

[1] See p. 38, n. 1.

[2] Cf. Ibn Hishām, p. 152 . ' So the Prophet went forth to Hirā ', as he was wont to do . . . '

[3] Sc. the Quraysh.   [4] Q v, 71.

[5] Cf. Ibn Hishām, p. 328.   [6] See p. 32, n. 3.

[7] To perform the " lesser pilgrimage ". Cf. Ibn Hishām, pp. 740 ff.

trial was ended, and victory came : how he entered Mecca, slaying and converting whom he wished, and then he published an amnesty in the city.[1] At that time God revealed : ' Surely We have given thee a manifest victory, that God may pardon thee thy former and thy latter sin '.[2]

So it was with Moses, and the place which he had with God. Consider how great was his trial, when he was still in his mother's womb, how the women were slaughtered, and the children slain, as they sought for Moses [3] Then his trial was visited upon the people, and God declared · ' And on the morrow he was afraid in the city, expectant ' [4] God also says : ' Verily, the chiefs are deliberating concerning thee, to kill thee . wherefore go forth Verily, I am for thee a sincere adviser So he went forth therefrom, afraid and expectant. He said, O Lord, save me from the unjust people ' [5]

Consider also, O disciple that seekest God's grace remissfully and with transgression ! Has it not been told thee, how that Moses did not obtain his wife, until he had guarded flocks and been a servant for ten years ? [6] Then God made him His messenger, and addressed him, and manifested his proof, saying ' Fear not: for I am with you twain, hearing and seeing ' [7] Now when God said to them, ' Do not fear ', did they fear ? Did he not make for them a sign, in the form of a rod, so that they were victorious over the wiles of the sorcerers, and put the armies to flight ? [8] Then God made him to prevail over his enemies, and drowned them altogether.[9]

So it was with Joseph, when, as God relates, he was cast into the pit,[10] and was then bought ' for a mean price, a few dirhams, and they parted with him cheaply ' [11] Then misfortune did not leave him, until he was tempted by the prince's wife,

---

[1] Ibn Hishām, pp. 802 ff.   [2] Q xlviii, 1-2.
[3] Cf. Q. xxviii, 3.   [4] Q. xxviii, 17   [5] Q. xxviii, 19–20
[6] Cf Q. xxviii, 25–29.   [7] Q xx, 48.
[8] Cf. Q. vii, 115   [9] Cf. Q. xx, 80.   [10] Cf. Q. xii, 15.
[11] Q. xii, 20.

and was imprisoned for many years.[1] But consider how God made him to prevail over (26a) his brethren for He drove them away, and manifested his proof, setting him over the treasures of the earth.[2]

So it was with the prophets, of whom God has spoken. This is surely eloquent to him who understands of God, and of those learned ones who are guides on the path unto God.

So it was with 'Umar ibn al-Khattāb. Of him it is related that, whatever path he trod, Satan trod another.[3] He said · ' Satan flees from 'Umar's brow, although yesterday he was engaged with al-Lātt and al-'Uzzā, on matters pleasing to Satan '. Consider how sincere he was to God, and judge truly whether the enemy and his lies had any part in him.

It is related that Thābit al-Banānī[4] said : ' I laboured with the Qur'ān twenty years, and have taken pleasure in it twenty years ' A philosopher said · ' These people persisted in the practice of patience, until it became honey [to them] '. Another said : ' Before every pious act is an obstacle · if a man boldly surmounts it, it will bring him to ease, but if he is afraid to surmount it, and does not pass over it, he remains in his place '."

I said : " And so there is no escape from this calamity and trial ? "

He replied : " There is no escape from it for the man who is highly esteemed of God, and has the gnosis of God. It is a true story of the Prophet that, being asked, ' Who of men suffers the most ? ', he replied : ' The prophets, then the righteous, then the like and the like '.[5] Every man is afflicted according to his religion. If there is a strength in his faith, his affliction is made more severe, but if his faith is weak, his affliction is lightened. So it was with the prophets. God revealed to them the grace of prophethood, and declared to them that they were apostles ; then He laid affliction on them, and they endured the affliction

---

[1] Cf Q xii, 23-35 [2] Cf Q. xii, 55.
[3] Cf. Wensinck, op. cit., p 234 [4] Died 123 h.
[5] Ibn Mājā, Fitan ch. 23, 2. Cf. Wensinck, op. cit., p. 197.

according to the grace which God had accorded them. With the affliction God schooled them, and they obtained understanding therein, and endured it patiently, until they were victorious.

All believers are affected firstly with a desire for God's reward which He has promised them, and secondly with a fear of the punishment wherewith He has threatened them. If they are patient, sincere, and truthful unto God, God is grateful to them therefor, and manifests their proof before all creation, making them learned men, patterns, and implanting in their hearts a sure faith. (26b) Thereafter believers fall into two classes. With the first, God makes beginning with blessing, favour, and gift, giving him repentance, making him to love penitence, and making obedience easy to him. So God makes beginning with abundant favours : then, when joy is fixed in his heart, and he finds pleasure in performing good acts, thereafter God lays upon him affliction and trial, calamities and hardship, difficulty and stress. Yes, and the sweetness, which formerly he tasted, and the joy in piety, these are taken from him : obedience becomes burdensome to him, though formerly it was easy, and he experiences bitterness after sweetness, sloth after alacrity, dullness after clarity : all this is by reason of the affliction and the trial. Then a weariness comes upon him. But if now he is steadfast and patient, and endures this unpleasantness, he afterwards comes to the bound of ease and attainment, and his grace is increased manifold, both outward and inward. So it is related in the Traditions : ' Every eagerness has its time of weariness : if a man's weariness turn him towards the Sunna, he is saved, but if it turn him to heresy, he perishes '.[1] Abū Bakr al-Ṣiddīq said : ' Blessed are they who died in the first flush of the beginning of Islam, and in its first eagerness '. It is related in the Traditions that God commands Gabriel, saying : ' Snatch away from My servant's heart

---

[1] Non-canonical, but cf. ' There is an eagerness for this Qur'ān, then men weary of it ' (Lane s.v. _shrr_).

the sweetness of obedience. If he mourns for it, return it to him, and give him an increase : if not, then leave him '.[1] In another Tradition it is related that God says : ' The least thing that I do with a man of learning, when he inclines to this world, is, that I remove from his breast the sweetness of secret converse with Me, and leave him in this world, bewildered '.[2] In another story it is said that, if a man inclines to this world after he has attained knowledge and gnosis, together with insight, God says to Gabriel : ' Remove from his breast the sweetness of secret converse with Me, and give him some fragment of this world, that he may occupy himself with it, and forget Me '.

As for the second man, he makes beginning with truthfulness and good acts and all the characteristics of truthfulness, then he practises therein as God wills : and thereafter grace comes to him, and God gives him what he had never hoped for or reckoned with. (27a) So it is with the majority of distinguished saints : signs and graces come not upon them, until they have practised, to the utmost of their power : when God makes beginning with them, He does not then accord them the greater part of what they had never reckoned with.

Some have studied the ways of these people, and then they are told, ' Surely thou art one of them ' ; and thereafter they have practised accordingly. Some know themselves, but do not know others Some know all by their names and tribes.

And so, O thou that enquirest concerning truthfulness and the exposition of the way, if thou hast duly learnt all that I have taught thee herein concerning truthfulness, if thou hast experienced these stages, lodged in these stations, and traversed these paths which we have mentioned, and therefrom passed to ease, repose and tranquility : then thou art hedged about with [divine] protection, and treadest the path of right conduct, and the white highway which brings thee to God. Mayst thou then find joy therein, and may God bless thee, for in all thy

---

[1] Non-canonical.   [2] Non-canonical.

ways thou hast a [true] insight   And if thou hast practised
truthfulness, and in every station acted with piety to the best
of thy powers, as much as God has permitted thee, and if thou
hast witnessed [all these] matters, then it may be that God has
seen thee, striving thy utmost in what passed between thee and
Him, because of thy desire to draw nigh to Him, so that thou
didst truly require Him, since thou knewest that thou must needs
have Him, and so thou camest to Him for protection   Or it
may be that God has seen thee at certain times seeking Him,
eager with truthful purpose and true aim, and He knew that
thou growest not weary, and leavest nothing undone, to turn
unto Him, until thou hast attained thy hope : then He showered
upon thee His goodness, and gave thee some part of thy hope of
Him—nay, He drew thy heart strongly unto Himself, and
implanted in it sure faith, making it to look upon the world to
come   Then indeed He makes easy for thee that which was
hard, and softens for thee that which thy soul found to be rough,
namely, submission ; then thy path unto Him is shortened, and
thy establishment is sure, thy life stands fast, and thy days
are blessed, for so the noble Master declares Himself, Who
suffers not diminution by His giving, and whose benefits never
end, because He is the Kind, the Compassionate, and He has
called Himself the Grateful.   (27b)

Then wonder of all wonders, and wonder of every wonderer !
Yet no wonder is it, for herein the noble Master was doing as
He desires . but this is indeed an occasion for men to marvel
at, that He is grateful to His servants for the very thing which
He began in them, guiding them unto it and employing them
in it and preserving them [in it] ; then He made it desirable
to them, and ascribed it to them as something done by them ,
then He inscribed it in their accounts as an accepted act ; then
He doubled for them the reward which He had promised them
for this   This, then, is the goodness which proceeds from the
generous [Lord] : this is not understood by men, for every mind
is amazed at it.

Ho then, O disciple who questionest! Awake from this long slumber. These are names which God has attached to them, [saying] that they were the agents these are matters which He has ascribed to them. Yet I do not think that this belongs to any other than God: this was His assistance, and His work, in a work which He alone originated, and He alone manifested when He wished. He performs all that He desires, and with His mercy visits whomsoever He wishes.

Men who understand of God meet all circumstances as I have described and set forth, and in all things return to Him · for they see that all things belong to Him ; for He was their inception, and on Him rests their completion, He is their supporter, and to Him they return God's is the command, both before and after · ' aye, His is the creation and the bidding , blessed be the Lord of the Worlds '.[1] But as for weak creatures, they imagine that herein is something which they have wrought Alas, if they are truthful and sincere, they seek a reward therefor from God, and that is as much as they know , and yet with God they have a great good

(He said) And I will mention to thee yet another station wherefore turn thyself attentively thereto, and any other man thou seest referring to gnosis and knowledge and repose in God If thou hast drunk the cup of the gnosis of God, if God has given thee to realize, through pure faith, what was already in eternity laid up for thee with Him—when He desired thee, before ever thou didst desire Him, knew thee before thou camest to a knowledge of Him, recollected thee before thou didst recollect Him, loved thee before thou lovedst Him—then now within thee gratitude is stirred for all his favours, now love cleaves to thy heart for all his favours. Him thou preferrest, and in Him thy spirit is rejoiced, and with His nearness thou art familiar Now thou comest unto Him taking refuge, and dwelling in nearness to Him : henceforward He will not be absent from thee, and

---

[1] Q vii 52.

thou wilt not lose Him, whether going or coming, (28a) standing or sitting, waking or sleeping, in every state.

Hast thou not heard what is related of the Prophet ? He said · ' Mine eyes sleep, but my heart does not sleep '.[1] So it is with all believers, according to their degrees. How glorious then is thy occupation, O man, and how splendid thy engagement ! For the Master, noble, great, exalted, rich, praiseworthy, has recollected thee again and again : thee He singled out, to shower on thee His amplest bounty, when He guided thee to love Him, so that thou didst prefer Him, and He became thy ambition and desire, and the object of thy yearning. Nothing that thou possessest is due to men, for all that thou hast is a gift [from God] This is the first sign of attaining to spiritual ease, that God should be the desire of His servants, God and none other. Now the sign of this is, that He preserves in thee that which He entrusted to thy heart—His recollection and His affection—making thee to feel how near He is, yearning over thee in His goodness, forgiving thee Now cease in thee all motions of desire to attain or to draw near · one motion only remains, which stirs within thee gratitude for His favours, payment of His due, association with Him and no other, pleasure in secret converse with Him, joy in His service, and such worship as He in His will desired of thee, that He might show thee wherein His power dwells, and how various are His ordinances to thee, and that thou mightest understand of Him. At that moment thou feelest how near He is to thee, for thou art no more occupied with thy own motions, nor seekest thou any reward or recompense therefor, as so many pious servants [of God] have desired : thou labourest more than abundantly for God, Who generously created thee, and has used thee in the character of generous men. God is [our] help.

This, then, is another answer to thy question, ' Does a man attain a state in which he no longer seeks to attain truthful-

---

[1] See Wensinck, *op. cit* , p. 163.

ness ? ' [1] This is the sign of those who do attain : do thou therefore understand it. Dost thou not know, disciple, that godliness, abstinence, patience, trust, fear, hope, respect, shame, love, yearning, intimacy, truthfulness and sincerity in all situations, every fair and lovely characteristic—all these are stations dwelt in by those who work for God, (28b) from which they depart to journey to others, until they have attained their desire, being near to their Master ? Then what hast thou to do with recollecting any station in which thou hast dwelt, until such time as it brought thee to thy goal, if thou hast now attained, and obtained some part of thy quest ? For it is as though thou hast Him in sight · wherefore ever more and more do thou advance towards Him, constantly gazing on Him, and listening to Him with ears attentive ; for He is nearer to thee than thyself to thy soul What then hast thou to do with recollecting truthfulness, which is but one of the stations of the seekers ?

And so, if now the door is opened, which was closed between thee and Him, if that veil is removed which once covered thy heart, if He has caused thee to feel Him near to thee, and has delighted thee with some degree of intimacy, then it may be that thou hast come to some part of thy request, and thy establishment is firm. But if thou, like certain other seekers, hast come no more to seek after truthfulness and like matters, because God's nearness is so real to thee that thou art wholly occupied with Him, then this is the desire of those who possess the gnosis of God : do thou understand it, both in thyself and in others, and be not deceived as to the portion thou hast from thy Lord.

Know, then, that those who have attained unto God, and are near to Him, who have in truth tasted the love of God, and obtained their portion from their King, their qualities are : godliness, abstinence, patience, sincerity, truthfulness, trust, confidence, love, yearning, intimacy, all fine characteristics, all the characteristics of theirs which cannot be described,

---

[1] See p. 53, n. 1.

together with that piety and generosity which they have made
their abode. All this is with them, dwelling in their natures,
hidden in their souls : nothing else find they good, for this is
their food and their habitude This they imposed on themselves as a duty, and therein practised, until they became familiar
with it. after they had attained, they no longer felt the per-
formance and practice of this to be a labour, since it dwelt [in
them] at every time and in every state—for this was their food—
even as in the discharge of their religious duties they experienced
neither heaviness nor exertion (29a) so overwhelmed were
their hearts by God's preference and nearness To practise
this was no burden to them, and it entailed no preoccupation
with outward acts for service and outward acts only affect the
outward members. Understand well this point Thereafter
their hearts were wholly oblivious—nay, they were wholly
occupied with God. for God's nearness overmastered them, and
His love, the yearning after Him, and the fear of Him, reverence
for Him, and respect Understand therefore, O disciple, what
I have set before thee, and meditate it well, and thou wilt find
it clear and agreeable, if God wills

Summon now thy intellect, and concentrate thy purpose [1] :
listen no more to knowledge, for thou hast turned away thy
understanding from all that knowledge puts before thee After
this knowledge and this exposition, there no longer remains any
excuse for thee, for the proof has been reiterated to thee Act
therefore in true sincerity unto God, that haply thou mayst be
saved, and rejoice in the true knowledge of Him in this abode,
fleetingly, before the [coming of the] eternal. Yea, and then
will thy sorrow be perpetual, and thy anguish redoubled, and
every spiritual state intensified many times above that which
thou didst experience before the coming of gnosis and attainment.

Now the verification of this may be found in God's Book,
and in the practice of His Prophet God says : ' So none fears

---

[1] Cf. Sarrāj, Kitāb al-Luma', p. 355, where this phrase is ascribed
to Kharrāz.

God of His servants save those who know '.[1] The Prophet said :
' I have most knowledge of God out of all of you, and of you all
I fear Him the most ' [2] He also said . ' If ye knew what I know,
ye would laugh little and weep much, and ye would go forth
on the highways boldly unto God '.[3] So lived the Prophet :
and so lives every man who knows God truly , though he be
near to material things, in every state in which he dwells he is
assisted by what he experiences therein, contrary to the use of
other men On this analogy then [understand it] . surely this is
eloquent to him who understand and meditates. God is [our]
help "

I said · " When does a man become familiar with his
Master's decrees, and find satisfaction in His disposition and
choice ? "

He replied : " As to this matter, men are in two stations, so
do thou understand The first man only becomes familiar with
his Master's decrees (29b), in order so to perform His command
as to attain His reward : this is good, and in it is great advantage ;
but such a man rises and falls, now is patient now impatient,
now pleased now angry, now crosses now reverts , this indeed
brings him to God's reward and mercy, but only with trouble,
hardship and labour. The second man becomes familiar with
his Master's decrees, and finds pleasure in His afflicting, being
satisfied with His good disposition and choice, entirely and without reserve for he is familiar with his Master and the recollection of Him, loving Him and cherishing Him, and being
pleased and content with Him. Can the decree of the Beloved, O
questioner, ever be a burden to the lover ? Will he not accept it
with joy and delight ? The story runs . ' Until he reckons
affliction a blessing, and ease a misfortune ' [4] In another story
we are told ' The booty of sincere believers is what they have
been deprived of in this world '.[5] It is related that God in one

---

[1] Q. xxxv, 25.

[2] Non-canonical

[3] Bukhārī, Kusūf ch. 2.

[4] Non-canonical.

[5] Non-canonical.

of His books revealed : ' O all ye who turn lovingly unto Me !
Ye shall not be harmed by what ye obtain of this world, for I
am your fortress . and ye shall not be harmed by any man's
enmity, for I am your deliverance '. If a man stands thus
with God in all states and situations, how can it be otherwise
with him than as we have mentioned ?

A certain man who knew God, and lived near to Him, has
said : ' These people, whose states we have been mentioning,
are not satisfied that they should have to contend with affairs
as they occur to them, and events as they come upon them, and
then, when the events take charge of their hearts, find it necessary
to be patient or pleased with them. In their case patience and
pleasure are an appositive adjunct [1] : having required of themselves that they should be truly occupied with God, and wholly
taken up with Him, they are not satisfied that passing events
should contend with their recollection of God, and even equal
it ; ' for God can overcome His affair '.[2] Moreover, they are
servants under God's decree : only on the very rarest of occasions
are they overcome, so that they need to confess their weakness
to God, (30a) and ask Him for help ' Marvel not, therefore, if
thou seest aught of this in any of them ; for so the Prophet
said ' Verily I am a man. O God, whomsoever I curse, let
my curse be to him a mercy '.[3] I heard a man who knew God
say . ' It is a proof of a man being strongly attached to his
Master, and enjoying real experience of Him in nearness to
Him, that he does not notice the varying conditions that pass
in him he looks at them with an inward eye, so that it seems
as if they are befalling or happening to someone else '. This is
the most perfect way of meeting changing conditions. Understand therefore this point, and meditate upon it, for it will
bring thee to the knowledge of repose in God, if God wills.

Repose in God, and tranquillity, are in proportion to the
heart's nearness. This is the explanation of the heart reposing

---

[1] The grammatical terms *tābi'* and *muḍāf* are used.

[2] Q xii, 21.

[3] Aḥmad ibn Hanbal, V, p. 294.

in God : that the heart loses all sense of material things, that the incitements of personal purpose are quiet, and that the mind is tranquil with God and unto God.   Then it is that all matters pertaining to this world and the next, all deeds of piety and obedience, actually seek out the man, and attach themselves to him (for they have need of him), and join him ; or rather, they are joined with him : for he has turned himself from them, being satisfied with Him Who possesses them [all], so that they may be said to join him.[1]   God says : ' Is not God enough for His servant ? '[2]   We are told that God revealed to Jesus : ' Set Me within thee in the place where thy purpose is, and make Me thy treasure in Paradise '.   It is related of the Prophet, on more than one authority, that he said . ' Whoso makes his purpose a single purpose, God suffices him for all his purposes '[3]   It is related that al-Fuḍayl ibn 'Iyāḍ said : ' I do not wonder at the worship of an angel that has been brought near [to God], or of a prophet sent [by God], for it is God Who has given them the power to do this '.   So it is with these people whose qualities we have mentioned.   Now if a man judges God's servants by himself and his own standard, or by themselves and their like, they always seem to him to be somewhat wanting : why then should he marvel, if he judges them by God's standard, in accordance with His power and dispensation ?   God is [our] help." (30b)

A Point which Proves what We have Said

I said · " What sayest thou concerning the following ? There was a man who neither spoke, nor moved, nor did anything at all, without feeling that there was something required of him therein, and that there was somewhat wanting.   Then a weariness and hardness [of heart] came upon him, whenever he obtained anything, or ate or drank aught, or in whatever state he chanced to be.   Then he passed to a state in which he spoke,

---

[1] Sc. as good acts to be credited to him at the Judgment

[2] Q. xxxix, 37   [3] See p. 24, n. 1.

and moved about his business, closing and opening his hands, eating and drinking, without feeling any dismay, and without any sense of a demand being made on him, or of being in any way wanting, as was the case before."

He replied : " This is an excellent question, so apply thy understanding to it : how great is the need for it in practising disciples !   Know that the disciple who is seeking after truthfulness acts in all his affairs in the fear of God, keeping watch over his heart, his purpose, and his members, and examining them. He concentrates his purpose, being afraid lest aught which concerns him not should enter into it, and being afraid of heedlessness, lest his bodily motions as manifested in his external members cause him to be somewhat wanting, and lest the purposes which enter inwardly into his heart perturb his [single] purpose.   Thus he frees himself from all such motions, even if they be right and proper . for his heart is overwhelmed by an urgent desire that his recollection [of God] shall be perpetual, and his purpose single. If he continues thus, his heart gains a quick understanding, and his thoughts become clear, and light lodges in his heart   he draws near to God, and God overwhelms his heart and purpose. Then he speaks, and his heart surges with the recollection of God : the love of God lurks deeply hidden in his inmost heart, cleaving to his mind, and never leaving it.   Then his soul is joyfully busied with secret converse with God, and passionate study, and ardent talk.   So he is, eating, or drinking, or sleeping,[1] in all his motions : for when God's nearness takes possession of a man's heart, it overwhelms all else, (31a) both the inward infiltrations of the purposes and the outward motions of the members.   Therein that man continues, going or coming, taking or giving · there prevails in him the purpose which has ruled his mind, namely, the love of God and His nearness.

Hast thou not marked, O disciple, how that sometimes the heart is subjected to a purpose connected with this world's

---

[1] Probably we should add ' or waking '.

affairs, and that it robs thee of everything, so that thy life becomes darkened, and thou forgettest all else but this, and even losest thy sleep over it ?   But God's command is more suitable and proper for the intelligent man.   In all that we have mentioned, a man is accompanied by divine protection, so that he is preserved from all shortcoming.   Understand, therefore, O questioner, this that is set before thee, and meditate thereon, and it will profit thee, if God wills.

And now do thou set what I have said to thee side by side with thy question.   If it suffices thee, and if it is the sort of thing which thou hast lost or found, then thank God, and He will give thee an increase   Hidden not from the learned is this that is passing within thee, for there is no hypocrisy between the disciple and his master, if God wills.   Truly I am an instructor of insight and wit, in this our time.   God is [our] help.''

INDEX OF PROPER NAMES.

Lightning Source UK Ltd.
Milton Keynes UK
UKHW051256160522
402993UK00013B/107

كتاب الصدق

للشيخ أبي سعيد الخرّاز

قدّس الله روحه ونوّر قبره

بسم الله الرحمن الرحيم

الحمد لله واسلام على عباده الّذين اصطفىٰ، قال الشيخ الامام
العارف ابو سعيد احمد بن عيسى البغدادي الخرّاز قدّس الله
روحه ونوّر ضريحه قلت لبعض العلماء اخبرني عن الصّدق كيف
هو وما معناه وكيف العمل به حتّى اعرفه ، فقال الصّدق اسم
للمعان كلّها وهو داخل فيها اتحبّ ان اجيب عن مسألتك جوابا
مختصرا اجمله ام اشرح لك العلم والعمل بالاصول التي بها
تقوم الفروع ، قلت اريد الامرين جميعا ليكون ذلك عِلما
لي وفقها ونصرة ، فقال وفّقت إن شاء الله

اعلم انّه لا بدّ للمريد المحقّق في ايمانه والطالب لسلوك
سبيل النّجاة من معرفة ثلاثة اصول يعمل بها فبذلك يقوى
ايمانه وتقوم حقائقه وتثبت فروعه فتصفو عند ذلك
الاعمال وتخلص ان شاء الله ، فاوّلها الاخلاص لقول الله
عزّ وجلّ فَاعْبُدِ اللّهَ مُخْلِصًا لَهُ الدِّينَ أَلَا لِلّهِ الدِّينَ
الْخَالِصُ وقال تعالى فَادْعُوا اللّهَ مُخْلِصِينَ لَهُ الدِّينَ
وقال لمحمّد صلّى الله عليه وسلّم قل إِنِّي أُمِرْتُ أَنْ

له للمعاني

أَعْبُدُ ٱللَّهَ مُخْلِصًا لَهُ ٱلدِّينَ وقال قُلِ ٱللَّهَ أَعْبُدُ مُخْلِصًا لَهُ
دِينِي وقال جل ذكره وَٱذْكُرْ فِي ٱلْكِتَابِ مُوسَى إِنَّهُ كَانَ مُخْلِصًا
وَكَانَ رَسُولًا نَبِيًّا ونحو هذا فى القرآن كثير وفي هذا مقنع،
ثم الصِّدق لقول الله عزوجل يَا أَيُّهَا ٱلَّذِينَ آمَنُوا ٱتَّقُوا
ٱللَّهَ وَكُونُوا مَعَ ٱلصَّادِقِينَ وقال تعالى فَلَوْ صَدَقُوا ٱللَّهَ
لَكَانَ خَيْرًا لَهُمْ وقال تعالى رِجَالٌ صَدَقُوا مَا عَاهَدُوا
ٱللَّهَ عَلَيْهِ وقال تعالى وَٱذْكُرْ فِي ٱلْكِتَابِ إِسْمَٰعِيلَ إِنَّهُ
كَانَ صَادِقَ ٱلْوَعْدِ وقال لِيَسْأَلَ ٱلصَّادِقِينَ عَن صِدْقِهِمْ
وقال تعالى وَٱلصَّادِقِينَ وَٱلصَّادِقَاتِ وهذا كثير فى القرآن
ثم الصبر لقول الله عزوجل يَا أَيُّهَا ٱلَّذِينَ آمَنُوا ٱصْبِرُوا وَ
صَابِرُوا وقال تعالى وَلَئِن صَبَرْتُمْ لَهُوَ خَيْرٌ لِّلصَّابِرِينَ (٦)
وَٱصْبِرْ وَمَا صَبْرُكَ إِلَّا بِٱللَّهِ وقال تعالى وَٱصْبِرْ لِحُكْمِ
رَبِّكَ فَإِنَّكَ بِأَعْيُنِنَا وقال تعالى وَٱصْبِرْ عَلَى مَا يَقُولُونَ
وَٱهْجُرْهُمْ هَجْرًا جَمِيلًا وقال تعالى وَٱصْبِرْ نَفْسَكَ مَعَ
ٱلَّذِينَ يَدْعُونَ رَبَّهُم بِٱلْغَدَاةِ وَٱلْعَشِيِّ يُرِيدُونَ وَجْهَهُ
وقال تعالى وَٱصْبِرُوا إِنَّ ٱللَّهَ مَعَ ٱلصَّابِرِينَ وقال تعالى
وَبَشِّرِ ٱلصَّابِرِينَ نجعل لهم الكرامة بالبشرى وهذا كثير

مُوَحِّد فى القرآن

وهذه ثلاثة أسام لمعانٍ مختلفة وهي داخلة في جميع الأعمال ولا تتمّ الأعمال إلا بها فإذا فارقت الأعمال فسدت ولم تتمّ ولا يتمّ بعض هذه الأصول الثلاثة الا ببعض فمتى فُقِد أحدها تعطّلت الأُخَر (قال) فالإخلاص لا يتمّ إلّا بالصدق فيه والصبر عليه والصبر لا يتمّ إلّا بالصدق فيه والإخلاص فيه والصدق لا يتمّ الا بالصبر عليه والإخلاص فيه ، فأوّل الأعمال هو الإخلاص فالفرض الواجب أن تؤمن بالله وتعلم وتقرّ وتشهد الا اله الا الله وحده لا شريك له وأنّه ٱلۡأَوَّلُ وَٱلۡأٓخِرُ وَٱلظَّٰهِرُ وَٱلۡبَاطِنُ الخالق الباري المصوّر الرازق المحي المميت الذي اليه تُرۡجَعُ ٱلۡأُمُورُ وأنّ محمّداً عبده ورسوله جاء بالحقّ من عند الحقّ والنبيّين حقّ وبالحقّ أدّوا الرسالة وبالغوافى النصيحة وأنّ الجنّة حقّ والبعث حقّ والمردّ الى الله تعالى يَغۡفِرُ لِمَن يَشَآءُ وَيُعَذِّبُ مَن يَشَآءُ ، ويكون ذلك عقدك ظاهراً على لسانك بلا شكّ ولا ريب ساكنٌ قلبُك مطمئنٌ الى ماصدّقت به وأقررت ، وكن لك لا يعارضك في كل ماجاء من له اسامى عك لمعانى عك مخمد عك وظاهر

.

عند الله على لسان نبيّه صلى الله عليه وسلّم شكّ في كل ما

ذكره عن ربّه عزّ وجلّ غير مخالف لما كان عليه النبي صلى

الله عليه وسلّم وأصحابه وأئمّة الهدى الذين كانوا قدوة

لمن جاء بعدهم من أهل الهداية ثمّ التابعون من بعدهم

ثمّ علماء كل عصر متّبعًا للجماعة مخلصًا في ذلك لله وحده

لا تريد الا الله تعالى ليتمّ اسلامك وايمانك وتوحيدك

باب الصدق فى الاخلاص الثانى (٭) وهو الذي امر

الله تعالى به حين يقول فَمَنْ كَانَ يَرْجُوا لِقَاءَ رَبِّهِ فَلْيَعْمَلْ

عَمَلًا صَالِحًا وَلَا يُشْرِكْ بِعِبَادَةِ رَبِّهِ أَحَدًا، فمن شرح

ذلك أن يكون العبد يريد الله عزّ وجلّ بجميع اعماله و

افعاله وحركاته كلّها ظاهرها وباطنها لا يريد بها الا الله

وحده قائمًا بعقله وعلمه على نفسه وقلبه راعيًا لهمّه

قاصدًا الى الله تعالى بجميع أمره لا يحبّ مدح احد ولا ثناءه

ولا يفرح بعمله اذا اطلع عليه المخلوقون فان عارضه من

ذلك شئ اتّقاه بالسرعة والكراهية ولم يسكن اليه لكن

اذا أثنى عليه احد حمد الله على ستره عليه حين وقّقه لخير

رآه العباد عليه ، نعم ثمّ يخاف عند ذلك من عمله الردي

لله التابعين لله متبع

وسريرته القبيحة التى خفيت على النّاس ولم تخف على الله فأشفق من ذلك وخاف أن تكون سريرته أقبح من علانيته، فهكذا يروى فى الحديث السريرة اذا كانت أقبح من العلانية فذلك الجور فاذا استوت السريرة و العلانية فذلك العدل واذا فضلت السريرة على العلانية فذلك الفضل

فالواجب على العبد أن يخفى عمله جهده حتى لايطّلع عليه الاّ الله تعالى فذلك أبلغ فى رضاء الله عزّوجلّ وأعظم فى تضعيف الثواب وأقرب الى السلامة واوهن لكيد العدو وأبعد من الآفات ، وروى عن سفيان الثورى رحمه الله أنه قال ما أعبأ بما يظهر من عملى ، ويروى فى الحديث أن عمل السّر يفضل على عمل العلانية سبعين ضعفا ، ويروى أن العبد ليعمل العمل فى السّر فيدعه الشيطان عشرين سنة ثمّ يدعوه الى أن يظهره ويذكره فينقل من ديوان السّر الى ديوان العلانية فينقص من ثواب العمل وفضله ثمّ لا يزال يذكّره أعماله حتى يذكرها للناس ويتحلّى اطلاعهم عليها ويسكن الى ثنائهم فيصير رئاء

له وينحلّا

فهذه الامور ضدّ الاخلاص وما ذكرنا فهو جملة الاخلاص
الّذي لابدّ للمخلوقين من معرفته والعمل به ولا يسعهم
جهله ، وتبقى (٧) الزيادة فى الاخلاص مع العبد اذا أحكم
هذه الاصول ،، قلت ثمّ ماذا قال ممّا يمكن أن يذكر أن
يكون العبد لا يرجوا الا الله ولا يخاف الا الله ولا يتزيّن
الا الله ولا يأخذه فى الله لومة لائم ولا يبالى اذا وافق الامر
الذى فيه محبّة الله ورضاه من سخطه ، وما بقى من ذكر
غاية الاخلاص أكثر و فى هذا بلاغ للمريدين السالكين للطريق
باب ثمّ الصدق فى الصبر، والصبر اسم لمعان ظاهرة
وباطنة ، فأمّا الظّاهرة فهى ثلاث فأوّلها الصبر على اداء
فرائض الله تعالى على كل حال فى الشدّة والرخاء والعافية و
البلاء طوعا وكرها ، ثمّ الصبر الثانى وهو الصبر عن كل ما
نهى الله تعالى عنه ومنع النفس من كل ما مالت اليه بهواها
ممّا ليس لله تعالى فيه رضاً طوعا وكرها، وهذان صبران فى
موطنين هما فرض على العباد أن يعملوا بهما ، ثمّ الصبر الثالث
وهو الصبر على النوافل وأعمال البرّ ممّا يقرّب العبد الى الله
تعالى فيحمل نفسه على بلوغ الغاية منه للذى رجاه من
له لمعانى الله والبلى لله رضى

ثواب الله عزّ وجلّ ، وهكذا يروى أنّ النبيّ صلّى الله عليه
وسلّم فيما رواه عن ربّه عزّ وجلّ قال ما تقرّب الى عبدى
بمثل ما افترضته عليه ولا يزال عبدى يتقرّب الىّ بالنّوافل
حتّى أحبّه ، والصبر الرابع وهو الصبر على قبول الحقّ ممّن
جاءك به من النّاس ودعاك اليه بالنصيحة فيقبل منه لأن
الحقّ رسول من الله جلّ ذكره الى العباد ولا يجوز لهم ردّه
فمن ترك قبول الحقّ وردّه فانّما يردّ على الله تعالى امره ،
وهذا ظاهر الصبر الواجب على الخلق الذى لا يسعهم جهله
ولا بدّ لهم منه وبقى شرح حقائق الصبر وغايته الذى
يكون مع الصابرين بعد إحكام هذا الصبر الذى ذكرناه

قلت فالصبر فى نفسه ما هو وما موجوده فى القلب قال
الصبر هو احتمال مكروه النفس وموجوده اذا وقع (٭)
بالنفس ما تكرهه تجرّعت ذلك وأنفت الجزع وتركت
البثّ والشكوى وكتمت ما نزل بها ، لأنّه يروى فى
الحديث من بثّ فقد شكا ، ألم تسمع الله تعالى يقول وَ
ٱلۡكَاظِمِينَ ٱلۡغَيۡظَ وَٱلۡعَافِينَ عَنِ ٱلنَّاسِ أفلا ترى أنّه
كظم ما كره وشقّ على نفسه احتماله فصار صابرا ، فاذا

أبدى الجزع وكان أما من أساء اليه ولم يعفّ عمّن أساء اليه يخرج
من حدّ الصبر على هذا القياس

قلت فيما أذا يقوى الصابر على الصبر وبماً أذا يتمّ له
قال يروى فى الحديث أنّ الصبر على المكاره من حسن
اليقين ويروى أنّ الصبر نصف الايمان واليقين الايمان
كلّه ، وذلك أنّ العبد لما أمن بالله تعالى وصدّق قوله
فى الذى وعده وتواعده قامت فى قلبه الرغبة فى ثواب
الله تعالى الذى وعده ولزمت قلبه الخشية من عقاب
الله الذى تواعده وصحّت عند ذلك رغبته وقامت
عزيمته فى طلب النّجاة ممّا يخافه وهاجت أماله فى
الظفر بالذى يرجوه فجدّ عند ذلك فى الطلب والهرب
فسكن الخوف والرجاء قلبه فركب عند ذلك مطيّة الصّبر
وتجرّع مرارته عند نزوله ومضى فى انفاذ العزائم و
حذر من نقصها فوقع عليه اسم الصبر

باب والصدق اسم لمعان كثيرة فأوّل الصدق هو
صدق العبد فى الانابة الى الله تعالى بالتوبة النّصوح لقول
الله عزّ وجلّ يَا أَيُّهَا ٱلَّذِينَ آمَنُوا تُوبُوا إِلَى ٱللَّهِ تَوْبَةً
له يفوا له فيما له وبما له لمعانى

نَصُوحًا وقال تعالى وَتُوبُوا إِلَى اللهِ جَمِيعًا أَيُّهَ الْمُؤْمِنُونَ لَعَلَّكُمْ تُفْلِحُونَ وقال تعالى لَقَدْ تَابَ اللهُ عَلَى النَّبِيِّ وَالْمُهَاجِرِينَ وَالْأَنْصَارِ، فأوّل التّوبة هو النّدم على ما كان من التفريط فى امر الله تعالى ونهيه والحزيمة على ترك العود فى شىء ممّا يكره الله عزّ وجلّ ودوام الاستغفار وردّ كلّ مظلمة للعباد من مالهم وأعراضهم والاعتراف لله تعالى ولهم و لزوم الخوف والحزن والاشفاق (٨) ألّا تكون مصحّحاو الخوف أن لا تقبل توبتك ولا تأمن أن يكون قد رأى ك الله تعالى على بعض ما يكره فمقتك، وهكذا يروى عن الحسن البصرى رضى الله عنه أنّه قال ما يؤمنى أن يكون قد رأى نى على بعض ما يكره فقال اعمل ما شئت فلا غفرت، و يروى عنه أيضاً أنّه قال أخاف أن يطرحنى فى النار ولا يبالى، وبلغنى أن بعض العلماء لقى بعض النّاس فقال له تبتَ قال نعم قال قُبلتَ قال لا أدرى قال أذهب فادرى، وقال يفنّى حزن كل ثكلى وحزن التائب ما يفنّى

ومن صدق التوبة ترك الاخدان والاصحاب الَّذِينَ أعانوك على تضييع امر الله تعالى والهرب منهم وأن تتّخذهم

لك ايها ته وهكذى ته يفنا ته والذين

أعداء أو يرجعوا الى الله ، فهكذا قال الله عزّوجلّ ٱلۡأَخِلَّاءُ
يَوۡمَئِذِۭ بَعۡضُهُمۡ لِبَعۡضٍ عَدُوٌّ إِلَّا ٱلۡمُتَّقِينَ ، ومن صدق
التوبة خروج المأثم من القلب والحذر من خفايا التطلع الى
ذكر شيء ممّا أنبت الى الله منه ، قال الله عزّوجلّ وَذَرُوا
ظَاهِرَٱلۡإِثۡمِ وَبَاطِنَهُ ، واعلم أن المؤمن كلّما صحّ و
كثر علمه بالله تعالى دقّت عليه التوبة أبداء ألا ترى أن
النبي صلّى الله عليه وسلّم يقول إنّه ليغان على قلبي فأستغفر
الله وأتوب اليه كل يوم مائة مرّة ، فمن طهر قلبه من
الآثام والادناس وسكنه النور لم يخف عليه ما يدخل
قلبه من خفي الأنة وما يلزمه من القسوة من الهمّة بالزلّة
قبل الفعل فيتوب عند ذلك

باب ثمّ الصدق فى معرفة النّفس والقيام عليها ، قال
الله عزّوجلّ يَٰٓأَيُّهَا ٱلَّذِينَ ءَامَنُوا۟ كُونُوا۟ قَوَّٰمِينَ بِٱلۡقِسۡطِ
شُهَدَآءَ لِلَّهِ وَلَوۡ عَلَىٰٓ أَنفُسِكُمۡ أَوِ ٱلۡوَٰلِدَيۡنِ وَٱلۡأَقۡرَبِينَ
وقال تعالى فى قصة يوسف عليه السّلام حين يذكرعنه
وَمَآ أُبَرِّئُ نَفۡسِىٓ إِنَّ ٱلنَّفۡسَ لَأَمَّارَةٌۢ بِٱلسُّوٓءِ إِلَّا مَا رَحِمَ
رَبِّى وقال تعالى وَأَمَّا مَنۡ خَافَ مَقَامَ رَبِّهِۦ وَنَهَى ٱلنَّفۡسَ

عَنِ ٱلۡهَوَىٰ فَإِنَّ ٱلۡجَنَّةَ هِىَ ٱلۡمَأۡوَىٰ ، وقال رسول الله صلّى
الله عليه وسلّم أعدى عدوّلك نفسك التى بين جنبيك
ثمّ أهلك ثمّ ولدك ثمّ الأقرب فالأقرب، (٭) ويروى عنه
صلّى الله عليه وسلّم أنه قال نفس إن قبقبها ونعمتها ذمّته
غدا عند الله قيّل له وماهى قال أنفسكم التى بين جنبيكم،
فمن صفة الصادق فى القصد الى الله تعالى أن يدعو نفسه
الى طاعة الله تعالى وطلب مرضاته فان أجابته حمد الله
تعالى وأحسن اليها، فهكذا يروى عن أبى هريرة رضى الله
عنه أنّهم رأوه يوطّئ شيئا يقترّشه فقيل له ما هذا قال
نفسى إن لم أحسن اليها لم تحملنى، وإن لم تجبه الى ما
يرضى الله ورأها بطيئة منعها محبوبها من العيش مخالفها
عند ما تهوى وعاداها فى الله ولله وشكاها الى الله حتى
يصلحها له ولا يقيم على ذمّها مع الاحسان اليها وذكر عيوبها
والله م لها وما لا يرضاه من فعلها مع الاقامة معها على الذى
تهواه من الفعل ، وهكذا يروى عن بعض العلماء أنه قال
قد علمت أنّ من صلاح نفسى على بفسادها وكفى بالمرء اثما
أن يعرف من نفسه عيبا لا يصلحه وليس منتقلا من ذلك

له اعلم ٭ ناقص فى الاصل

الى توبة ، وقال بعض العلماء إن كنت صادقا فى ذمّك لنفسك
فان ذمّك غيرك بما فيك فلا تغضب

واذا نازعتك نفسك الى شئ من الشهوات أو شغل
قلبك فى طلب شئ متا حرم عليك وحلّ لك فاتهمها تهمة من
يريد صلاحها وامنعها من ذلك منع من يريد استعبادها واحملها
بالامتناع عن الملاذ علّى اللحوق بمن تقدّمها فانّ الذى نازعتك
اليه لا يخلو من أن يكون حراما تستحقّ به السخط أو حلالا
تستوجب به طول الوقوف على المسائلة اذا امضى التا ركون
للحرام اجلالا له وتعظيما له ووقفوا عن الحلال للا نكماش
والمبادرة ، فاعمل فى فطام نفسك عن الحالين جميعا فانّ من
فطم نفسه عن الدنيا كان رضاعه من الاخرة ومن اتّخذ الأخرة
أمّا أحبّ برّها والورود عليها اذا رضى أبناء الدنيا بالدنيا
أمّا وبرّوها وسعوا من أجلها فارم المؤثرين للدنيا من قلبك
بالهجران مع النّصيحة لهم (٩) وتحذيرهم ايّاها واحذر
التّخلّف عن السابقين وانظر فى خاصّة نفسك وحثّ على
ذلك أصفياءك وبطائنك فانّ السابقين شمروا وشدّوا
المآزر وكشفوا عن الرؤوس والسوق فاغتنموا الصحّة و

له عن   له المآزر

بادروا فى النشاط ورعواحقّ الله تعالى أن يهتكوا سترا ممّا
نهاهم عنه وتجنّبوا اليه برفض ما أباح لهم أخذه وتركوا
الحرام تعبّدا والحلال تقرّبا وألفوا السهر والظمأ وأنسوا الى
التبلّغ والاجتزاء باليسير

باب ثمّ الصدق فى معرفة عدوّك ابليس، قال الله عزّ
وجلّ إِنَّ ٱلشَّيْطَانَ لَكُمْ عَدُوٌّ فَٱتَّخِذُوهُ عَدُوًّا إِنَّمَا يَدْعُوا
حِزْبَهُ لِيَكُونُوا مِنْ أَصْحَابِ ٱلسَّعِيرِ وقال جلّ وعزّ يَا
بَنِي آدَمَ لَا يَفْتِنَنَّكُمُ ٱلشَّيْطَانُ كَمَا أَخْرَجَ أَبَوَيْكُمْ
مِنَ ٱلْجَنَّةِ وقال تعالى وَزَيَّنَ لَهُمُ ٱلشَّيْطَانُ أَعْمَالَهُمْ
فَصَدَّهُمْ عَنِ ٱلسَّبِيلِ، وقال عبد الله بن مسعود رضى الله
عنه للملك لمّة وللشيطان لمّة فلمّة الملك ايعاد بالخير
ولمّة الشيطان ايعاد بالشرّ، وقال فى خبر آخر إنّ الشيطان
جاثم على قلب ابن آدم فاذا ذكر الله خنس واذا غفل وسوس
فاقطع مادّته بالعزيمة على مخالفة هواك ومنع نفسك من
الافراط والتشوّف فهما خير أعوانه عليك وبهما يقوى كيده
واذا اتّبعتهما فأحضر عقلك وعلمك الذى علّمك الله تعالى
فقم بهما على نفسك وراع قلبك وما يقع فيه فما كان من

له عدوا

أجناس الخير والعلم فاتّبعه وما كان من جنس الباطل والهوى
فانفه بالسرعة ولا تماد على الخطرة فتصير شهوة ثمّ تصير
الشهوة همّة ثمّ تصير الهمّة فعلا واعلم أنّ عدوّك ابليس
لا يغفل عنك فى سكوت ولا كلام ولا صلوة ولا صيام ولا بذل
ولا منع ولا سفر ولا حضر ولا تفرّد ولا خلطة ولا فى توقّر ولا
عجلة ولا فى نظر ولا فى غضّ بصر ولا فى كسل ولا فى نشاط
ولا فى ضحك ولا فى بكاء ولا فى إخفاء ولا فى إعلان (*) و
لا حزن ولا فرح ولا صحّة ولا سقم ولا مسئلة ولا جواب ولا
علم ولا جهل ولا بعد ولا قرب له ولا حركة ولا سكون ولا
توبة ولا إصرار، ولن يألو جهدا فى توهين عزمك وفتور نيّتك
وتأخير توبتك ويسوّف بترك قتال الى وقت ويأمرك بتعجيل ما
لا يضرّك تأخيره يريد بذلك قطعك عن الخير ثمّ يذكّرك
فى وقت شغلك بالبرّ والطاعة الحوائج ليقطعك عن خير
أنت فيه، وربّما حبّب اليك النقلة من بلد الى بلد يوهمك
أنّ غير البلد الذى أنت فيه أفضل ليشغل قلبك ويعطل
مقامك بما يعقبك الندم اذا أنت فعلته
فاحترس من عدوّك أشدّ الاحتراس وتحصّن منــه

ـه ولا قتور زائد فى الاصل

بالملجأ الى الله عزّوجلّ فانّه أمنع الحصون وأقوى الاركان
فاجعل الله تعالى كهفك وملجأك واحذر رعدوك عند
الغضب والحدّة فانّك ان استقبلك فى هيج الغضب ذكر
الله تعالى وعلمت أنّه شاهدك بمراقبته نيران العزّ أطفأت
وتوقّد الحمية وأجللت من قد علمت أنّه يراك من أن تحدث
فى غضبك ما استحقّ به غضبه فانّ الشيطان يغنم منك هيج
الغضب وحمّية الشهوة، وأما احذرك ايّاه عند الحدّة فانّه يقال
انّ الشيطان يقول انّ الحديد من العباد لن نأيس منه ولو كان
يحيى بدعائه الموتى لانّه تأتى عليه ساعة يحتدّ فنصير منه
الى ما نريد ومن يعتصم بالله فقد هدى الى صراط مستقيم
باب ثمّ الصدق فى الورع واستعمال التقيّة، فالصدق فى
الورع هو الخروج من كلّ شبهة والترك لكلّ ما اشتبه عليك
من الامور، فهكذا يروى عن النبى صلّى الله عليه وسلّم أنّه
قال لا يكون العبد من المتّقين حتى يدع ما لا بأس به مخافة ما
به بأس، وقال صلّى الله عليه وسلّم الحلال بيّن والحرام بيّن وبين ذلك
امور مشتبهات، (١٠) فمن ترك الشبهات مخافة أن يقع فى الحرام فقد
استبرأ عرضه، وقال ابن سيرين رحمة الله عليه ما فى دينى شىء
لله اطفيت لله وحموة لله حلال لله وحرام

أيسر من الورع كل ما اشتبه عليك تركته، وقال الفضيل رحمه
الله يقول الناس الورع شديد دع ما يريبك الى ما لا يريبك
نخذ ما حل وطاب من الاشياء وابذل المجهود فى طلب الشئ
الصافى من الحلال لأن الله عزّ وجلّ قال يَا أَيُّهَا الرُّسُلُ كُلُوا
مِنَ الطَّيِّبَاتِ وَاعْمَلُوا صَالِحًا، وقال النبى صلى الله عليه
وسلّم لسعد رضى الله عنه إن أردت أن يجيب الله تعالى
دعاءك فكل الحلال وقالت عائشة رضى الله عنها يا رسول
الله من المؤمن قال من اذا أمسى نظر من أين قرصه

باب ثمّ الصدق فى الحلال الصافى اذا وجدته وكيف
العمل به، فالصدق فى الحلال اذا وجدته أن تأخذ منه
ما لا بدّ منه على قدر معرفتك بنفسك وما يقيم ميلها ولا
تحمل عليها فوق طاقتها فتنقطع ولا تصير معها الى ما تهواه
من السرف ولكن خذ ما يقيمك بلا تفتير ولا سرف فى الطعام
واللباس والسكن واحذر الفضول مخافة الحساب وطول
الوقوف، فهكذا يروى أنّ رجلا قال لعلى بن أبى طالب رضى
الله عنه يا أبا الحسن صف لنا الدنيا فقال حلالها حساب و
حرامها عذاب أو عقاب، فاذا كان العبد ضعيفا ثمّ ملك الشئ

الطيّب حبسه على نفسه وعلى من يمون فانفق منه بالمعروف
منافاة أن يكون اذا أخرجه لم يصبر وجزع فوقع فى ما هو
أردى منه منكان فى حبسه ايّاه مزريا على نفسه من اتّخاره
حين عدم من نفسه الثقة بالله تعالى والسّكون اليه دون
الشئ فيكون كذلك حتى يقوى عزمه

قلت فكيف ملك الانبياء عليهم السلام الاموال و
الضياع مثل داود وسليمن وابراهيم وأيّوب ونظرائهم و
يوسف عليه السلام على خزائن الارض (۞) ومحمّد صلّى
الله عليه وسلّم والصالحين من بعد، فقال هذه مسئلة
كبيرة وفيها كثيرا اعلم أنّ الانبياء عليهم السّلام والعلماء
والصالحين من بعد هم رضى الله عنهم أمناء الله تعالى فى
ارضه على سرّه وعلى امره ونهيه وعلمه وموضع وديعته
والنصحاء له فى خلقه وبريّته وهم الذين عقلوا عن الله
تعالى امره ونهيه وفهموا الما ذا خلقهم وما ارادا منهم وإلى
ما ندبهم فوافقوه فى محبّته ونزلوا فى الامور عند مشيئته
ثمّ وقفوا عند ذلك مواقف العبيد الألبّاء القابلين عن الله
والحافظين لوصيّته وأصغوا اليه بأذان فهومهم الواعية و
له كبير

قلوبهم الطاهرة ولم يتخلّفوا عن ندبته فسمعوا الله عزّ وجلّ يقول آمنوا بالله ورسوله وَأَنْفِقُوا مِمَّا جَعَلَكُمْ مُسْتَخْلَفِينَ فِيهِ ثم قال ثُمَّ جَعَلْنَاكُمْ خَلَائِفَ فِى ٱلْأَرْضِ مِنْ بَعْدِهِمْ لِنَنْظُرَ كَيْفَ تَعْمَلُونَ وقال تعالى لِلَّهِ مَا فِى ٱلسَّمَوَاتِ وَمَا فِى ٱلْأَرْضِ وقال تعالى أَلَا لَهُ ٱلْخَلْقُ وَٱلْأَمْرُ، فأيقن القوم أنهم وأنفسهم لله تعالى وكذلك ما خوّلهم وملّكهم فانّما هو له غيرُ أنهم فى دار اختبار وبلوى وخلقوا للاختبار و البلوى فى هذه الدار، وهكذا يروى عن عمر بن الخطاب رضى الله عنه حين سمع هَلْ أَتَى عَلَى ٱلْإِنْسَانِ حِينٌ مِنَ ٱلدَّهْرِ لَمْ يَكُنْ شَيْئًا مَذْكُورًا قال يا ليتها تمّت يعنى عمر قبل قراءة إِنَّا خَلَقْنَا ٱلْإِنْسَانَ مِنْ نُطْفَةٍ أَمْشَاجٍ نَبْتَلِيهِ فهمهم ـ يقال فى التفسير عجز فى التلاء عجزا ـ ومعنى قول عمر رضى الله عنه يا ليتها تمّت يعنى لم يخلق حين سمع الله تعالى يقول لَمْ يَكُنْ شَيْئًا مَذْكُورًا وذلك من معرفة عمر رضى الله عنه بواجب حقّ الله و قد رامره ونهيه وعجز العباد عن القيام به وقيام الحجّة لله تعالى عليهم عند تقصيرهم وما تواعد هم به اذا ضيّعوا،

ويروى عن الحسن رضى الله عنه أنه قال إن الله تعالى اتما أهبط أدم عليه السلام الى الدّنيا عقوبة وجعلها سجنا له حين أخرجه من جواره وصيّره الى دار التعب والاختبار ويروى فى الحديث أنّ الله لتاخلق ادم قبل أن ينفخ فيه الروح فعلم الله تعالى ما يكون (١١) من ذرّيته أراد أن يبحقه، قال الشّيخ أبو سعيد رحمه الله قال رجل من البدلاء النبلاء رحمه الله ليته محقه ولم يخلق

فمن ملك من أهل العمل عن الله تعالى وأهل الصدق شيئا من الدنيا فهو معتقد أن الشئ لله جلّ وعزّلا له الّا هو من طريق حقّ ما خوّله الله تعالى وهو مُبلى به حتى يقوم بالحقّ فيه لأنّ النعمة بلاء حتى يقوم العبد بالشكر فيها ويستعين بها على طاعة الله تعالى وكذلك البلوى والضراء هو اختبار وبلاء حتى يصبر عليه ويقوم بحقّ الله تعالى فيه، وكذلك قال بعض الحكماء العلم كلّه بلاء حتى يعمل به، قال الله عزّ وجلّ الَّذِى خَلَقَ الْمَوْتَ وَالْحَيٰوةَ لِيَبْلُوَكُمْ وقال وَلَنَبْلُوَنَّكُمْ حَتّٰى نَعْلَمَ الْمُجَاهِدِينَ مِنْكُمْ وَ الصَّابِرِينَ وَنَبْلُوَا أَخْبَارَكُمْ، فالانبياء صلوات الله

عليهم والصالحون من بعد هم الذين أشعرهم الله بأن
أبلاهم في الدنيا بالسعة وخوّلهم كانوا الى الله جلّ وعزّ
ساكنين لا الى الشئ وكانوا اخذّ انا لله جلّ ذكره في الشئ الذي
ملّكهم ينفذونه في حقوق الله تعالى غير مقصرين ولا
مفرطين ولا متوانين ولا متأوّلين على الله التاويل وكانوا
غير متلذّذين بما ملّكوا ولا مشغولين القلوب بما ملكوا
ولا مستأثرين به دون عباد الله تعالى، ومن ذلك ما روى
عن سليمن بن داود عليهما السلام في ملكه وما أباحه
الله تعالى من الكرامة حين يقول تعالى هٰذَا عَطَاؤُنَا
فَامْنُنْ أَوْ أَمْسِكْ بِغَيْرِ حِسَابٍ قال أهل التفسير لا حساب
عَلَيْكَ في الآخرة وانّما كان عطاء مهينا إكراما من الله عزّ
وجلّ له، فذكر العلماء أنّ سليمن عليه السلام كان يطعم
الاضياف الحواري النقي ويطعم عياله الخشكا ويأكل
هو الشعير وكذلك روى العلماء أنّ ابراهيم الخليل صلوات
الله عليه كان لا يأكل الّا مع الضيف فربّما لا يأتيه ثلاثة
أيام الضيف فيطويها وربّما كان يمشى الفرسخ أو أقلّ أو
أكثر تلقّيا للضيف (٭) قال وكان أيّوب النبي صلّى الله

عليه وسلّم لا يسمع أحدًا يحلف بالله تعالى الّا رجع الى منزله
فكفّر عنه، وروى العلماء أنّ يوسف عليه السّلام كان
على خزائن الأرض فكان لا يشبع فقيل له فى ذلك فقال
أخاف أن أشبع فأنسى الجياع، ولقد روى أنّ سليمن عليه
السّلام بينا هو ذات يوم والريح تحمله والطير تظلّه والجنّ
والانس معه وعليه قميص جديد فلصق ببدنه فوجد اللّذّة
فسكنت الريح ووضعته على الارض فقال لها مالك قالت
اتّما أمرنا أن نطيعك ما أطعت الله ففكّر فى نفسه من أين
أتى فذكر فراجع فحملته الريح ولقد روى أنّ الريح كانت
تضعه فى اليوم مرّات من هذا وأشباهه

فالقوم كانوا خارجين من ملكهم فى ملكهم ناعمين
بذكر الله وعبادته غير ساكنيّن الى ما ملكوا لا يستوحشون
من فقده إن فقدوه ولا يفرحون بالشئ ولا يحتاجون الى
العلاج والمجاهدة فى إخراجه، قال الله تعالى للنّبى صلى
الله عليه وسلّم أُولَٰئِكَ ٱلَّذِينَ هَدَى ٱللَّهُ فَبِهُدَاهُمُ ٱقْتَدِهْ
وهذا النبى صلى الله عليه وسلّم سما جبريل عليه السّلام
عنده اذ تغيّر جبريل فاذا ملك قد نزل من السماء لم ينزل

<hr>

لله ناقص فى الاصل ‏ للله شاكنين

قط فقال جبريل عليه السلام خشيت أنه نزل فىّ بأمر فجاء
الى النبى صلى الله عليه وسلم بالسلام من عند الله عزّ وجلّ
وقال له هذه مفاتيح خزائن الارض تسير معك ذهبا وفضة
مع البقاء فيها الى يوم القيامة ولا تنقصك ممالك عند
الله شيئا فلم يختر النبى صلى الله عليه وسلم ذلك وقال
أجوع مرّة وأشبع مرّة ، وعدّ ذلك من الله عزّ وجلّ بلوى و
اختبارا ولم يره من الله تعالى اختيارا ولو كان من الله تعالى
اختيارا لقبله ولكنه علم أن محبّة الله تعالى فى الترك
للدنيا والاعراض عن زينتها وبهجتها ، وبذلك أدّ به الله
تعالى حين قال تعالى (١٢) وَلَا تَمُدَّنَّ عَيْنَيْكَ إِلَىٰ مَا مَتَّعْنَا
بِهِ أَزْوَاجًا مِّنْهُمْ زَهْرَةَ ٱلْحَيَوٰةِ ٱلدُّنْيَا لِنَفْتِنَهُمْ فِيهِ، و
يروى عنه صلّى الله عليه وسلم أنه لبس حلّة لها علم
فطرحها وقال كادت أن تلهينى أعلامها ۔ أو قال ألهتنى
أعلامها ۔ خذوها واتوفى بأَنْبِجانيّة ، وكذلك روى أنه
صُنع له خاتم ذهب ليختم به الكتب الى مَن امره الله تعالى
بانذاره فلبسه ثمّ طرحه من يده وقال لاصحابه اليه
نظرة واليكم نظرة ، وكذلك روى أنه صلّى الله عليه وسلم
له يختار مِّ واحتبار

غيّر شراك نعله فجعل مكانه جديد فقال ردّوا الشراك
الأوّل .

وكذلك كلّ قلب طاهر صاف قد اشرف على الاخرة
وعرف قيام الله تعالى عليه يفزع من خفايا السكون الى الدّنيا
والتحلّي بشئ منها ومثل هذا في الاخبار كثير والعاقل الفطين
تكفيه الاشارة اليه بالشئ ، وهذا اصحاب محمّد صلّى
الله عليه وسلم حين حثّهم على الصدقة جاء ابوبكر بماله
كلّه لأنه كان أقوى القوم فقال له النبي صلّى الله عليه وسلّم
ما خلّفت لعيالك قال الله ورسوله ولي عند الله مزيد، أفلا
ترى أبا بكر رضى الله عنه انّما كان سكونا الى الله تعالى
لا الى الشئ ولم يكن لشئ عنده قدر وكان ما عند الله عنده
أسترّ فحين رأى موضع الحقّ لم يخلف منه شيئا وقال خلّفت
الله ورسوله ، ثمّ جاء عمر رضى الله عنه بنصف ماله فقال
النبي صلّى الله عليه وسلم ما خلّفت لعيالك قال نصف مالى
ولله عندى مزيد فقد أعطى نصف ماله ويقول ولله عندئ
ثمّ عثمان رضى الله عنه يجهّز جيش العسرة كلّه بجميع ما
يحتاج اليه ويحفر بئر رومة، أفلا ترى أن القوم انّما كانوا
لله صافى

معتدين الشئ لله تعالى ومِمّا يدلّ على صدق قولنا ان القوم كانوا خارجين ممّا ملكوا وهو فى ايديهم يعدّ ونّه لله عزّ وجلّ (٭) وقد روى عن النبى صلى الله عليه وسلّم أنه قال إنّا معاشر الانبياء لا نورّث وماخلّفناه صدقة ، أفلا ترى أنهم رفضوا فى حيوتهم لم يضنّوا بالشئ عن الله عزّ وجلّ وكذلك لم يورّثوه وخلّفوه لله عزّ وجلّ كما كان فى أيديهم لله تعالى لم يحدثوا فيه ولم يخوّلوه من بعدهم أحدا ، وإنّ هذا لَبَلاغٌ لمن عقل عن الله تعالى وأنصف من نفسه

وهذا أئمّة الهدى بعد رسول الله صلّى الله عليه وسلّم أبو بكر رضى الله حين ملك الامر وجاءته الدنيا راغمة مِن حِلّها لم يرفع بها رأسا ولم يتصنّع وكان عليه كساء يخلّله وكان يدّعى ذو الخلالين ، وهذا عمر بن الخطاب رضى الله عنه حين جاءته الدنيا راغمة من حلّها وكان طعامه الخبز والزيت وُفِى ثوبه بضع عشر رقعة بعضها من أدم وقد فتحت عليه كنوز كسرى و قيصر، وهذا عثمان رضى الله عنه كأ نه واحد من عبيده فى اللباس والزيّ ولقد روى عنه أنه رؤى خارجا من بستان

له يعدوه لله لبلاغا لله يدعا

له وعلى عنقه حزمة من حطب فقيل له فى ذلك فقال
أردت أن أنظر نفسى هل تأبى، أفلا ترى أنه كان غير
غافل عن نفسه وتعاهدها ورياضتها، وهذا على بن أبى
طالب رضى الله عنه فى الخلافة قد اشترى ازارا بأربعة
دراهم واشترى قميصا بخمسة دراهم فكان فى كمّه
طول فتقدّم الى خرّاز فأخذ الشفرة فقطع الكمّ مع أطراف
أصابعه وهو يفرق الدنيا يمنة ويسرة، وهذا الزبير
رضى الله عنه يخلّف حين مات من الدين مائتى ألف أو
أكثر كل ذلك من الجود والسخاء والبذل، وهذا طلحة
بن عبيد الله رضى الله عنه يعطى حلى أهله لمن سأله،،
فهذا يدل أن القوم كانوا كما قال الله عزّ وجلّ حين امرهم
فقال وَأَنْفِقُوا مِمَّا جَعَلَكُمْ مُسْتَخْلِفِينَ فِيهِ ، ولا
يستحيى عبد من عبيد الله من اهل (١٣) زمانتاه هذا
عند ما ملك من الشبهات التى علم الله تعالى كيف هى و
من أين هى وكيف قدرها فى قلبه وايثاره لها وسكونه اليها
دون الله عزّ وجلّ وما لا يحصى من عيبه فى تقلّبه فى ذلك
واشتغاله بذلك حتى أن أحدهم ليزعم أنه يملك كما
له تابا

ملك من مضى ويحتجّ بهم فى اتّباع هواه مع اقامته على
خلاف سنّة القوم، بل الاعتراف لله تعالى بالتقصير من
العبد الغافل أقرب الى النجاة وسؤاله الله عزّوجلّ أن
يبلغه ما بلغه بالقوم وبالله التوفيق

باب ثمّ الصدق فى الزهد وكيف هو وما هو، ولقد
فضح الله تعالى الدنيا وسمّاها بأسماء لم يسمّها أحد
فقال تبارك وتعالى أَنَّمَا الْحَيَوةُ الدُّنْيَا لَعِبٌ وَلَهُوٌ وَزِينَةٌ
وَتَفَاخُرٌ بَيْنَكُمْ الآية أَفَلَا يستحيى مِمّن يعقل عن الله
تعالى أن يراه ساكنا الى اللّهو واللعب فى دار الغرور، قلت
الدنيا فى نفسها ما هى قال اتّفق البصراء من الحكماء أن
الدنيا هى النفس وما هويت والحجّة فى ذلك أنّ الله عزّ
وجلّ قال زُيِّنَ لِلنَّاسِ حُبُّ الشَّهَوَاتِ مِنَ النِّسَاءِ وَالْبَنِينَ
وَالْقَنَاطِيرِ الْمُقَنْطَرَةِ مِنَ الذَّهَبِ وَالْفِضَّةِ وَالْخَيْلِ الْمُسَوَّمَةِ
وَالْأَنْعَامِ وَالْحَرْثِ ذَلِكَ مَتَاعُ الْحَيَوةِ الدُّنْيَا، فهذه
الامور التى ذكرها الله عزّوجلّ هى من هوى النفس لأنّها
وبها تلهو عن الآخرة وذكرها، فاذا ترك العبد ما تهواه
النفس ترك الدنيا ألا ترى أن العبد قد يكون فقيرا لا شئ
له فلا لله عند

له وهو يتمنّى الدنيا ويهوى مجناها وينوى أن لو أمكنه
منها ما يريد لتمتّع بذلك ونال لذّته فهو عند الله تعالى من
الراغبين على قدر همّته إلّا أنّه أقلّ حسابا ممّن نالها واستمتع بها.

فأوّل درجات الزهد هو الزهد في اتباع هوى النفس فاذا
هانت على المرء نفسه لم يبال على أيّ حال امسى وأصبح اذا
وافق محبّة الله تعالى (*) عند ذلك على مخالفة نفسه و
منعها من محبوبها من الشهوات واللذّات والراحات ومقارنة
الأحبّاء والاخدان والاصحاب من اهل الغفلة إلّا من كان
منهم عونا على ذلك الامر الذي يريده العبد فانّ أفة العبد
صحبة من يريد ما يريد، ثمّ أخذ البلغة من الطعام والشراب
واللباس والمنزل والنوم والكلام والنطق والاستماع و
ترك التمنّى لشئ من الدنيا والحذر من تحلّيها لانّ النبيّ
صلّى الله عليه وسلّم قال الدنيا حضرة حلوة، فيتوهّم العبد
فناءها فيقصر فيها أمله مع توقّع الموت والتشوّف الى
الآخرة والشوق الى النزول في دار بقائها والعمل في ذلك
ولذلك يخلع الراحة من القلب بدوام الفكرة ومن
البدن بدوام الخدمة فهذا أوّل درجات الزهد، وقال

سفيان الثورى رحمه الله تعالى ووكيع بن الجرّاح وأحمد
بن حنبل وغيرهم رحمهم الله إنّ الزهد فى الدنيا قصر
الآمال، وهذا يدلّ على ما قالت الحكماء لأنّه من قصر
أمله لم ينعم وكانت الغفلة منه بعيدة، وقالت طائفة
من الناس الزاهد فى الدنيا هو الراغب فى الآخرة الذى
قد جعلها نصب عينه كأنّه يرى عقابها وثوابها فهو
عازف عن الدنيا، وهكذا يروى أن النبى صلى الله عليه
وسلم قال لحارثة كيف أصبحت يا حارثة قال مؤمنا
حقّا يا رسول الله فقال النبى صلى الله عليه وسلّم وما
حقيقة ايمانك قال عزفت نفسى عن الدنيا فأظمأت
لذلك نهارى وأسهرت ليلى وكأنّى انظر الى عرش ربّى
بارزا وكأنّى انظر الى اهل الجنّة يتناعمون والى اهل
النار يتعاوون فقال النبى صلى الله عليه وسلّم مؤمن
نوّر الله قلبه عرفت فالزم، وقال بعض العلماء الزهد
خروج قيمة الاشياء من القلب، والزهد فى الدنيا يدقّ
جدّا ويخفى ولكلّ عبد (١٤) على قدر علمه بالله تعالى
زهد فمن نفى الرغبة فى الدنيا عن قلبه شيئا بعد شىء

له ويخفا

حتى يرى غاية الزهد ومن توانّى عن نفسه ولم يخالفها
عند هواها لم يعزف عنِّ الدنيا ولم يشرف على الآخرة، قال
بعض العلماء الزاهد في الدنيا حقًّا لا يذمّ الدنيا ولا يمدحها
ولا يفرح بها اذا أقبلت ولا يحزن عليها اذا أدبرت، قال
أبو سعيد رحمه الله تعالى قال بعض البدلاء رحمهم الله
تعالى لا يكون زاهدًا مستكمل الزهد أو يستوى عنده
الحجارة والذهب ولا يستوى الحجارة والذهب حتى
يكون معه من الله تعالى آية فتحوّل الحجارة ذهبًا فعندها
يخرج قيمة الاشياء من قلبه، وسمعته يقول لم يستوّ
الحجارة والذهب عند أحد من الصحابة رضى الله عنهم
بعد رسول الله صلّى الله عليه وسلّم إلّا عند أبى بكر
رضى الله عنه

قلت فعلى أى معنى زهد الزاهدون قال على معانٍ شتى
فمنهم من زهد لفراغ القلب من الشغل وجعل همّته كلّه
فى طاعة الله تعالى وذكره وخدمته فكفاه الله عند ذلك،
فهكذا روى عن النبى صلّى الله عليه وسلّم أنه قال من
جعل الهمّ همًّا واحدًا كفاه الله سائر همومه، وقال عيسى

له توانا له ناقص فى الاصل له يستوى له معانى

عليه السلام بحقّ أقول لكم إنّ حبّ الدنيا رأس كلّ خطيئة وفى المال داء كبير قالوا يا روح الله ما داؤه قال لا يعطى حقّه قالوا فإن أعطى حقّه قال يكون فيه فخر وخيلاء قالوا فإن لم يكن فيه فخر ولا خيلاء قال يشغله استصلاحه عن ذكر الله، ومنهم من زهد لخفّة الظهر وسرعة المرّ على الصراط اذ احبس أصحاب الاثقال للسؤال، فهكذا روى عن النبى صلّى الله عليه وسلّم أنّه قال عرض علىّ أصحابى ففقدت عبد الرحمن بن عوف ــ أو قال احتبس علىّ ــ فقلت ما بطّأك علىّ قال لم أزل أحاسب بعدل مكثرة مالى حتى جرى منّى من العرق ما لو وردت (*) عليه سبعون من الابل عطّاش قد اكلت حمضا لصدرت عنه رواء، وروى عن النبى صلّى الله عليه وسلّم من غير طريق أنّه قال الاكثرون هم الاقلّون يوم القيامة إلّا من قال بالمال هكذا وهكذا عن يمينه وعن شماله ومن بين يديه ومن خلفه بين عباد الله، قال صلّى الله عليه وسلّم ما من غنىّ ولا فقير إلّا ودّ يوم القيامة أنّ الله تعالى كان جعل رزقه فى الدنيا قوتا، وروى أبو ذر عن النبى صلّى الله عليه

له بطاءك

وسلّم أنه قال ما يسرّني أن لى مثل أُحُد ذهباً أنفقه فى
سبيل الله تعالى تأتى علىّ ثالثة يكون منه عندى شئ إلّا
ديناراً أرصده لدين، ومنهم من زهد رغبة فى الجنّة و
اشتياقاً اليها فسلى عن الدنيا وعن لذّاتها حتى طال به
الشوق الى ثواب الله تعالى الذى دعاه اليه ووصفه له عزّ
وجلّ، وروى فى الحديث ان الله جلّ ذكره يقول وأمّا
الزاهدون فى الدنيا فإنّى أبيحهم الجنّة، وقال بعض العلماء
لا تحسن قراءة إلّا بزهد

وأعلى درجات الذين زهدوا فى الدنيا هم الذين وانفقوا
الله تعالى فى محبّته فكانوا عبيداً عقلاء عن الله عزّ وجلّ
أكياساً محبّين سمعوا الله جلّ ذكره ذمّ الدنيا ووضع
من قدرها ولم يرضها داراً لأوليائه استحيوا من الله عزّ
وجلّ أن يراهم راكنين الى شئ ذمّه ولم يرضه وجعلوا
ذلك على انفسهم فرضاً لم يبتغوا عليه من الله عزّ وجلّ
جزاءً ولكن وانفقوا الله فى محبّته كرماً والله لا يضيع أجر
من احسن عملاً، فأهل الموافقة لله تعالى فى الأمورهم
أعقل العبيد وأرفعهم عند الله قدراً، وهكذا روى عن

أبى الدرداء رضى الله عنه أنه قال يا حبّذا نوم الأكيا س
وإفطارهم كيف غنموا سهرالحمقى وصيامهم ولمثقال ذرّة
من صاحب تقوى ويقين أوزن عندالله من أمثال الجبال من
اعمال المغترّين، وفى هذا بلاغ لمن عقل (١٥) عن الله عزّ
وجلّ وبالله التوفيق، وروى عن عمر بن عبد العزيز رضى الله
عنه أنه نظر الى شابّ مصفرٍ فقال له ما هذا الصفار يا غلام
قال أسقام وأمراض يا أمير المؤمنين قال لتصدقنى قال
أسقام وأمراض قال لتخبرنى قال يا أمير المؤمنين عزفت
نفسى عن الدنيا فاستوى عندى حجرها وذهبها وكأن
انظر الى اهل الجنّة فى الجنّة يتزاورون وأهل النار فى
النار يتعاورون فقال له عمر انى لك هذا يا غلام قال اتّق
الله يفرغ عليك العلم افراغا إنّه لمّا قصرنا عن علم ما
عملنا تركنا العمل بما علمنا ولوعملنا ببعض ما علمنا
لورثنا علما لا تقوم له أبداننا، وروى عن أبى بكرالصدّيق
رضى الله عنه أنه استسقى فأتى بإناء فلمّا قرّبه الى فيه
وذاقه نحّاه ثمّ بكى فقيل له فى ذلك فقال رأيت رسول الله
صلّى الله عليه وسلّم ذات يوم وهويدفع بيده كأنّ شيئا

يقع ولا أرى شيئًا فقلت يا رسول الله أراك تدفع بيديك
ولا أرى شيئًا فقال نعم تلك الدنيا تمثّلت لى فى زينتها
فقلت اليك عنّى فقالت إن تنجو منّى ولن ينجو منّى من بعدك
قال أبو بكر رضى الله عنه فأخاف أن تكون قد أدركتنى
(قال) وكان فى الاناء الذى شرب أبو بكر رضى الله عنه منه
ماء وعسل فبكى اشفاقا من ذلك ، ويروى فى بعض الحديث
انّ اصحاب محمّد صلى الله عليه وسلّم لم يأكلوا تلذّذا
ولم يلبسوا تنعّما وفى رواية أن اصحاب محمّد صلى الله
عليه وسلّم الّذين اتّسعوا فى الدنيا من بعده حين فتحت
عليهم من حلها أنهم بكوا من ذلك وأشفقوا وقالوا نخاف
أن تكون عجّلت لنا حسناتنا ، فليتّق الله عبد ولينصف
من نفسه وليلزم منهاج من مضى وليعترف بالتقصير و
يسأل الله الإقالة

باب ثمّ الصدق فى التوكّل على الله عزّ وجلّ، (*) قال
الله عزّ وجلّ فَلْيَتَوَكَّلِ ٱلْمُؤْمِنُونَ وقال تعالى وَعَلَى ٱللَّهِ
فَتَوَكَّلُوا إِن كُنتُم مُّؤْمِنِينَ وقال تعالى إِنَّ ٱللَّهَ يُحِبُّ
ٱلْمُتَوَكِّلِينَ ، وروى عن النبى صلى الله عليه وسلم أنه

له فليتقى ﮑ وليعرف

قال يدخل الجنّة من أمّتى سبعون ألفا بغير حساب وهم
الذين لا يتطيّرون ولا يكتوون ولا يسترقون وعلى ربّهم
يتوكّلون، وقال عمر بن الخطّاب رضى الله عنه عن النبى
صلّى الله عليه وسلّم لو توكّلتم على الله حقّ توكّله لرزقكم
كما يرزق الطير تغدو خماصا وتروح بطانا، وقال عبد الله
بن مسعود رضى الله عنه العزّ والغناء يجولان فى طلب
التوكّل فاذا أصاباه أوطنا

فالتوكّل فى نفسه وموجوده فى القلب هو التصديق لله
عزّ وجلّ والاعتماد عليه والسكون اليه والاطمانينة اليه
فى كلّ ما ضمن وإخراج الهمّ من القلب بأمور الدنيا والرزق
وكلّ امر تكفّل الله به والعلم بأنّ كلّ ما احتاج اليه العبد
من امر الدنيا والآخرة فالله مالكه والقائم به لا يوصله اليه
غيره ولا يمنعه غيره مع خروج الرغبة والرهبة والخوف
من القلب ممّن سوى الله تعالى والثقة به والعلم الخالص
واليقين الثابت أن يد الله المبسوطة اليه الموفية له من
كل ما طلب فلا يصل اليه معروف إلّا من بعد امره ولا ينله
مكروه الا من بعد إذنه، وهكذا روى عن الفضيل أنه قال

المتوكّل على الله الواثق به لايتّهمه ولايخاف خذلانه، وكذلك المتوكّل على الله اذا ملّكه الله تعالى شيئًا من امر الدنيا وفضل عنده لم يذخره لغد إلّا بالنيّة أنّ الشئ اتّما هو لله وموقوف لحقوق الله وهو خازن من خزّان الله فاذا رأى موضع الحاجة سارع الى الاخراج والبذل و المؤاساة وكان فى الذى يملك وأخوانه سواء واتّما يجب ذلك عليه لأهل الستر خاصّة والقرابة وأهل التّقوى ثمّ لعامّ المسلمين اذا رأهم على حال ضرورة (١٧) غيّر نقص حالهم وروى عن النبى صلى الله عليه وسلّم أنه قال ليس الزهادة فى الدنيا بتحريم الحلال ولا بإضاعة المال ولكن الزهد فى الدنيا أن تكون بما فى يد الله أوثق منك بما فى يدك واذا أصابتك مصيبة كنت بثوابها أفرح منك لو بقيت عنك، وقال بلال رضى الله عنه جئت الى النبى صلى الله عليه وسلّم ومعى تمر فقال ما هذا فقلت شئ ادّخرته لافطارك فقال أنفق بلال ولا تخش من ذى العرش إقلالا أما خشيت أن يكون له بخار فى جهنّم ، ويروى عن عائشة رضى الله عنها أنها قالت إنى لست كأسماء ـ يعنى أختها ـ إن أسماء لاترفع

له عليك

شيئا لغد وأنا أجمع الشئ الى الشئ ، وروى عن عائشة أيضا
رضى الله عنها أنها فرقت الدراهم وهى ترفع درعها فقالت لها
خادمتها ألا أبقيت درهما للحم قالت فألا ذكّرتنى، وروت
عائشة رضى الله عنها عن النبى صلى الله عليه وسلّم أنه بات
فى مرضه الذى قبض فيه شبيه بالقلق فلمّا اصبح قال ما فعلت
الذهيبة ـ وكان قيمتها ستّة وخمسين درهما ـ فقال أخرجيها
فما ظنّ محمّد بربّه لو لقيه وهذه عنده ـ وروى عن مسروق
رحمة الله عليه أنه قال أوثق ما أكون بالله اذا قالت
الخادم ليس عندنا شئ

قلت فالتوكّل على الله تعالى بالاسباب أو يقطع الاسباب
قال بقطع أكثر الاسباب وتتخطّى الى السبّب فتسكن
اليه ، قلت وهل يتداوى المتوكّل أو يتعالج قال الامر
فى هذا على معان ثلاثة وقد خصّ تبارك وتعالى بترك الدواء
والاسباب طائفة لقول النبى صلى الله عليه وسلّم يدخل
الجنّة من أمّتى سبعون ألفا بلا حساب هم الذين لا يكتوون
ولا يسترقون وعلى ربّهم يتوكّلون وقال النبى صلى الله عليه
وسلّم ما توكّل من اكتوى واسترقى وقال صلّى الله عليه وسلّم
له وتتخطّا له واسترقا

(※) من ردّته الطيرة فقد قارن الشرك وقد امر النبي صلّى الله عليه وسلّم بالدواء والرُقى وأمر بالرقية وقطع لأبيّ بن كعب رضي الله عنه عرقا فهذا على معانى قول المغيرة بن شعبة لم يتوكّل من اكتوى واسترقى من هؤلاء السبعين ألف الذين خصّهم النبى صلّى الله عليه وسلّم كذلك فسّره بعض العلماء وما كان من سوى ذلك فمباح لهم من سائر الناس وهو غير ناقص من توكّلهم اذا كان معهم العلم والمعرفة و كان نظرهم الى ربّ الداء والدواء إن شاء أنْ ينفع بالدواء وإن شاء أن يضرّ وقد يطلب شفاءه بالدواء فيكون فيه سقمه وقد مات غير انسان من الدواء وقطع العرق ولمّا طلب الشفاء وقد يرجو منفعته فى الشئ فتكون فيه مضرّته وقد يخاف الضرر من شئ فتكون فيه المنفعة ، فالصادق واثق متوكّل على ربّه فانّما توكّل عليه حين علم أنه حسبه من جميع خلقه فلم يجد فقد شئ منعه الله لأن الله حسبه وهو بَالِغُ أَمْرِهِ

قلت فمن قال أتوكل على الله لأكفى قال لا يخلو هذا القول من معنين معنى أن يكفيه مُؤنة الجزع والهلع لا أنه

يتحوّل عنه شئ قد قدّره الله عليه أن ينزل به بالتوكّل
فهذا قولنا وقول من أثبت القدر ومن قال إنّه يكفيه ما
استكفاه لا محالة مثل قوله لا يأكلني السبع لتوكّلي و
الذى يأتيني بطلب يأتيني بلا طلب فالتوكّل يدفع عنّى
اذا استكفيته كل مؤنة كنت أخاف ها فليس يعجبنا هذا
القول لأن المتوكّل قد يكفى وقد لا يكفى وتوكّله غير ناقص

قلت مثل ماذا اشرح لى من ذلك شيئا قال نعم حيث
ذبحت يحيّى بن زكريّاء امرأة جبارة فى طشت لم يكن
متوكّلا وحين نشر زكريّاء صلوات الله عليه بالمنشار لم
يكن متوكّلا وكذلك الانبياء عليهم السلام قتلوا ونيل منهم
المكروه (١٧) وهم أقوى الخلق يقينا وأصدقه ، وهذا محمّد
صلّى الله عليه وسلّم حين هرب الى الغار هو وأبوبكر رضى
الله عنه فاختبوا فيه وحين كسر المشركون رباعيّته صلّى
الله عليه وسلّم وأدموا وجهه لم يكن متوكّلا ، أفلا ترى أن
التوكّل انّما هو الاعتماد على الله عزّ وجلّ والسكون اليه ثمّ
التسليم بعد ذلك لأمره يَفْعَلُ مَا يَشَآءُ ، وهكذا روى عن
عبدالله بن مسعود رضى الله عنه مَنْ يَتَوَكَّلْ عَلَى اللهِ فَهُوَ
له يكفا له من

حَسْبُهُ إِنَّ اللهَ بَالِغُ أَمْرِهِ قال قاض أَمَره قَدْ جَعَلَ اللهُ لِكُلِّ
شَيْءٍ قَدْرًا قال أجلاً ومنتهى ينتهى اليه العبد وليس المتوكّل
بالذى يقول تقضى حاجتى، فهذا تفسير ابن مسعود رضى الله
عنه يخبر أن المتوكّل على الله هوالذى يلجأ الى الله تعالى
ويعلم أنه لا يتمّ شئ إلّا من قبل الله تعالى الذى يُعْطى ويمنع
بقدرته فالمتوكّل على الله تعالى لا يستوحش فى حالة المنع
ولا يستجلب بالتوكّل الاعطاء لأن الحرص لا يعطى ولا يمنع
والله جلّ وعزّ ما نع ومعطى، وقد يعطى العبد الشىء بالتوكّل
ويمنع وهومتوكّل نقد يرى المجوسى والكافر والجاحد و
الفاجر المضيع لأمر الله عزّ وجلّ الذى لا صدق له ولا يقين
نقد يرى هازل يكفرون وتقضى لهم الحوائج والمتوكّل
الصادق الموقن لا تقضى له حاجة حتى يموت ضراء وهؤلاء،
وإنّما التوكّل ترك السكون الى أسباب الدنيا وإنفاء الطمع
من المخلوقين والاياس منهم حين علم المتوكّل أنه صائر
الى المعلوم فرضى بالله تعالى وعلم أنه لا يدرك بالتوكّل
تعجيل ما أخّر الله تعالى ولا تأخير ما عجّل ولكنه اكتسب
اسقاط الهلع والجزع واستراح من عذاب الحرص وراض
نفسه يعز

نفسه بأدب العلم والمعرفة وقال ماقد رسيكون وما يكون
فهواَتْ، وكذلك قال بعض الحكماء انتقم من حرصك بالقنوع
كما تنتقم من عدوّك بالقصاص، وقال بعض الصحابة رضوان
الله عليهم (ﷺ) دخلت على النبى صلّى الله عليه وسلّم وفى
البيت تمرة غابرة فقال خذها ولم تأتها لأتتك، حدّثنا
محمّد بن يعقوب قال حدّثنا أحمد بن حنبل قال حدّثنا مروان
بن معاوية قال حدّثنا المعلّى عن أنس بن مالك رضى الله
عنه قال أهدى الى النبى صلّى الله عليه وسلّم طوائر فأطعم
خادما طائرا فلمّا كان من الغد أتته به فقال ألم أنهك أن
تخبأ رزقا لغد، فهذا ما لا يسع الناس جهله من التوكّل و
غاية التوكّل اجلّ من ذلك

باب ثمّ الصّدق فى الخوف من الله عزّ وجلّ، قال الله تعالى
وَإِيَّايَ فَاتَّقُونِ وَإِيَّايَ فَارْهَبُونِ وقال تعالى فَلَا تَخْشَوُا
النَّاسَ وَاخْشَوْنِ وقال تعالى يَخَافُونَ رَبَّهُمْ مِنْ فَوْقِهِمْ
وقال تعالى كَذَلِكَ إِنَّمَا يَخْشَى اللهَ مِنْ عِبَادِهِ الْعُلَمَاءُ
وقال تعالى وَلَا تَعْمَلُونَ مِنْ عَمَلٍ إِلَّا كُنَّا عَلَيْكُمْ شُهُودًا
إِذْ تُفِيضُونَ فِيهِ وقال تعالى يَعْلَمُ مَا فِي أَنْفُسِكُمْ فَاحْذَرُوهُ،

له بادب العلم والمعرفة زائد فى الاصل

وقال النبى صلّى الله عليه وسلّم خف الله كأنّك تراه قال
ذلك لابن عبّاس رضى الله عنه، فالذى يهيج الخوف حتى
يسكن القلب هو دوام المراقبة لله عزّ وجلّ فى السّر والعلانية
وذلك لعلمك بأنّ الله تعالى يراك ولا يخفى عليه شئ من
حركاتك ظاهرا وباطنا فعند ذلك يجلّ مقامه عليك فى كلّ
حركة ظاهرة وباطنة وتحذر أن يرى بقلبك شيئا ممّا لا
يحبّه ولا يرضاه بالوقوف منك على همّك اذا كان ما
فى نفسك، فمن ألزم قلبه فى الحركات كلّها أنّ الله تعالى
يراه ورجع عن كل ما يكره بعون الله فطهر قلبه واستنار وسكنه
الخوف ودام حذره من الله فكان مشفقا فى جميع الأحوال و
عظم امر الله تعالى فى قلبه فلم تأخذه فى الله لومة لائم وقلّ
وصغر من دون الله فى عينه ممّن ضيّع أمر الله، وذكر الخوف
يطول وهذه الاصول التّى من استعملها تؤدّيه الى الحقائق
فهذا ظاهر الخوف وما بقى من صفته أكثر (۱۸)

باب ثمّ الصدق فى الحياء من الله عزّ وجلّ، يروى عن
النبى صلّى الله عليه وسلّم أنه قال الحياء من الايمان وروى
عنه صلّى الله عليه وسلّم أنه قال الحياء خيركلّه وقال

صلّى الله عليه وسلّم استحيوا من الله حقّ الحياء من استحيا
من الله حقّ الحياء فليحفظ الرأس وماحوى والبطن وما
وعّى وليذكر المقابر والبلى ومن أراد الآخرة ترك زينة
الدنيا وقال النبى صلّى الله عليه وسلّم استحى من الله
كما تستحيى من رجل صالح من قومك ، وقال رجل يا
رسول الله ما نبدى من عوراتنا وما نذر قال استرعورتك
إلّا من أهلك وما ملكت يمينك قال فأحد نا يكون خاليا
قال فالله أحقّ أن يستحيى منه ، وكان أبو بكر رضى الله عنه
اذا ذهب الى الخلاء يغطى رأسه ويقول إنّى لأستحيى من
ربّى ، وهذه أخبار تدلّ كلّها على قرب الله عزّ وجلّ من
القوم لأنّ المستحيى من الله تعالى يرى اطلاع الله تعالى
عليه ومشاهدته له فى جميع الاحوال

قلت فالذى يهيج الحياء قال ثلاث خصال دوام احسان
الله تعالى اليك مع تضييع الشكر منك ومع دوام اساءتك
وتفريطك ، والثانية أن تعلم أنّك بعين الله عزّ وجلّ فى
منقلبك ومثواك ، والثالثة ذكرك لوقوفك بين يدى
الله عزّ وجلّ ومسائلته ايّاك عن الصغير والكبير، قلت
له وعاه الله اذا ذكر له قلة (فوق)

فالذى يشيد الحياء ويقويه قال الخوف لله عزّوجلّ عند
الهوى الخاطر الواقع فى القلب فيفزع القلب ويستوحش عند
مايعلم أن الله تعالى يرى مافيه فيثبت الحياء من الله فاذا دام
على ذلك زاد الحياء وقوى ٌ قلت فالذى يولد الحياء ماهو قال
الفزع من أن يكون الله تعالى عنه معرضا وله ماقتا ولفعله غير
راضٍ ٌ قلت فالغالب على قلب المستحيى من ربّه لجلال رُؤية من
يراه فحينئذٍ يهاب الله عزوجلّ ويستحيى منه، (٭) قال أبوسعيد رحه
الله تعالى سمعت بعض المريدين سأل بعض أهل المعرفة قال ما
علامة هيبة الله فى قلب العارف بالله قال إذا استوى عنده الأفعى
والذباب، قلت فيم يضعف الحياء قال بترك المحاسبة
وترك الورع قلت فكيف أحوال المستحيى فى نفسه قال
طول الخشوع ودوام الاخبات وتنكّس الرأس وانحصار
الطرف وقلّة النظر الى السماء وكلال اللسان عن كثير
من الكلام والفزع من التكشّف فى الخلاء وترك العبث
والضحك والحياء عند اتيان ما أباحه الله، فكيف يذكر
عارض ممّا نهى الله تعالى عنه، والناس يتفاوتون فى
الحياء على قدر قرب الله تعالى منهم وقربهم منه

باب ثمّ الصدق فى معرفة نعم الله تعالى والشكر له،
قال الله عزّ وجلّ وَلَقَدْ كَرَّمْنَا بَنِى آدَمَ وَحَمَلْنَا هُمْ فِى
ٱلْبَرِّ وَٱلْبَحْرِ وَرَزَقْنَاهُمْ مِنَ ٱلطَّيِّبَاتِ وَفَضَّلْنَاهُمْ عَلَى
كَثِيرٍ مِمَّنْ خَلَقْنَا تَفْضِيلًا وقال تعالى وَإِنْ تَعُدُّوا
نِعْمَةَ ٱللَّهِ لَا تُحْصُوهَا وقال ٱذْكُرُوا نِعْمَتِيَ ٱلَّتِى
أَنْعَمْتُ عَلَيْكُمْ، فاذا أفاق العبد من الغفلة فكر و
نظر الى نعم الله تعالى عليه وتكاملها قديما وحديثا،
فأما نعمه القديمة فنذكره لك قبل أن تك شيئا وما
خصّك به من توحيده والايمان به والمعرفة له فأجرى
باسمك القلم فى اللوح المحفوظ مسلما ثمّ أهلك القرون
السالفة وجعلك فى شرذمة من المؤمنين ناجية حتى
أخرجك فى خير أُمّة وأكرم دين ومن أُمّته حبيبه محمّد
صلّى الله عليه وسلّم ثمّ هداك للسنّة واستعملك بالشريعة
وباعدك من الزيغ والأهواء ثمّ ربّاك وكلأك وغذاك حتى
وجبت عليك الأحكام فأغفلت نعمته وفرطت فى حفظ
وصيّته وركبت هواك من عمرك حينا وفى كل ذا ك لا يكافيك
بإساءتك بل يسترك ويحلم عنك وينظرك ثمّ عطف عليك

(١٩) بعد ذلك بعد ما كنت شرودا فأيقظك من الغفلة وعرّفك ما فاتك من حظك من طاعتك فوهب لك الانابة اليه وأجلسك على طيّب مرضاته نوجب عليك الأن شكر بعد شكر فأي نعماه تحصى وعلى أيتها تشكر ولا بدّ من معرفة الشكر ومباشرته ، والشكر على ثلاثة وجوه شكر القلب وشكر اللسان وشكر البدن فأما شكر القلب فهو أن تعلم أن النعم من الله وحده لا من غيره ، وأما شكر اللسان فالحمد والثناء عليه ونشر الآئه وذكر احسانه ، وأما شكر البدن فلا تستعمل جارحة أصحّها الله تعالى وأحسن خلقها في معصية بل تطيع الله تعالى بها وكذلك كلّ ما خوّلك و ملّكك من الدنيا جعلته عونا لك على طاعته ولم تحوّله في باطل ولم تنفقه في سرف ثمّ تبذل لله عزّ وجلّ ذكرى و عزّ جدّه الخدمة وتعطيه الجهد من نفسك ، وهكذا يروى عن النبي صلّى الله عليه وسلّم أنه قام حتى تورّمت قدماه فقيل له يا رسول الله ما هذا التعب أليس قد غفر الله لك قال أفلا أكون عبدا شكورا، وقال الله عزّ وجلّ إِعْمَلُوا أَلَ دَاوُدَ شُكْرًا وقال تعالى لَئِنْ شَكَرْتُمْ لَأَزِيدَنَّكُمْ ،

فاذا بلغ العبد من الشكر لله عزّ وجلّ غاية انقطع نظر فاذا
شكره نعمة من الله تعالى تحتاج الى أن يشكرالله تعالى
عليها اذجعله من الشاكرين فعمل عند ذلك فى شكرالشكر
ثمّ كاد أن يتحيّر تواترت عليه من الله تعالى الالطاف بالبرّ
والكرامات ، وبلغنا أنه فيما ناجى به موسى عليه السلام
ربّه عزّ وجلّ قال يا ربّ أمرتنى بالشكر على نعمتك وانّما
شكرى ايّاك نعمة من نعمك نأوحى الله اليه لقد علمت
العلم اذ علمت أنّ ذاك منّى فقد شكرتنى ، وقال عمر بن
عبد العزيز رضى الله عنه ذكر النعمة شكرا فادلّت (*)
النعم على محبّة المنعم

باب ثمّ الصدق فى المحبّة ، وقد أجمع الحكماء أنها
تستخرج من ذكرالنعم ، وروى عن ابن عباس رضى الله عنهما
عن النبى صلّى الله عليه وسلّم أنه قال أحبّوا الله لما يغذوكم
من نعمه وأحبّونى لحبّ الله وأحبّوا أهل بيتى لحبّى ، و
قال الله عزّ وجلّ وَالَّذِينَ اٰمَنُوٓا اَشَدُّ حُبًّا لِلّٰهِ ، وبلغنى
أنّ الله عزّ وجلّ أوحى الى عيسى عليه السلام يا عيسى بحقّ
أقول لك إنّى أحبّ الى عبدى المؤمن من نفسه التى بين

جنبيه ، وبلغنا عن الحسن البصري رضى الله عنه أنّ ناسا
قالوا على عهد رسول الله صلّى الله عليه وسلّم يا رسول الله
إنّا نحبّ ربّنا حبّا شديدا فجعل الله تعالى لمحبّته علما و
أنزل عزّ وجلّ فَإِنْ كُنْتُمْ تُحِبُّونَ ٱللّٰهَ فَٱتَّبِعُونِي يُحْبِبْكُمُ
ٱللّٰهُ ، فمن صدق المحبّة اتّباع الرسول صلّى الله عليه وسلّم
فى هديه وزهده وأخلاقه والتأسّي به فى الامور والاعراض
عن الدنيا وزهرتها وبهجتها فان الله عزّ وجلّ جعل محمّدا
صلّى الله عليه وسلّم علما ودليلا وحجّة على أمّته

ومن صدق المحبّة لله تعالى ايثار محبّة الله عزّ وجلّ
فى جميع الامور على نفسك وهواك وأن تبدر فى الامور كلّها
بأمره قبل أمر نفسك ، وبلغنا أنّ موسى عليه السّلام قال يا
ربّ أوصنى قال الله عزّ وجلّ أوصيك بى قال يا ربّ كيف
توصينى بك قال لا يعرض لك أمران أحدهما لى والآخر لنفسك
إلّا أثرت محبّتى على هواك ، فالمحبّ لله قد جعل ذكر الله
تعالى بقلبه ولسانه فرضا على نفسه فهو يتفرّغ من الغفلة
ويستغفر منها وكذلك جوارحه انّما هى وقف لخدمة من
أحبّه فهو غير ساهٍ ولا لاهٍ وإنّما همّته أن يرضى من أحبّه نقد

سه ساهى عله لاهى

بذل المجهود فى موافقته فى اداء فرائضه واجتناب مناهيه
فهو متزنتين له بكل طاقته حذرا من أن يأتى (٢٠) عليه أمر
يسقطه من عين من أجّه ، وهكذا روى عن النبى صلّى الله
عليه وسلّم من غير طريق أنه قال يقول الله عزّ وجلّ ما تقرّب
الى عبدى بمثل اداء ما افترضت عليه ولا يزال يتقرّب الىّ
بالنوائل حتى أحبّه فاذا أحببته كنت له سمعا وبصرا ويدا و
مؤيدا دعانى فأجبته ونصح لى فنصحت له ، فعلامة المحبّ
الموافقة للمجبوب والتجارىّ طرقاته فى كل الامور والتقرب
اليه بكل حيلة والهرب من كل ما لا يعينه على مذهبه

قلت فالمحبّة على قدر النعم قال المحبّة بدوها من ذكر
النعم ثمّ على قدر المنعم على قدر ما يستحقّ لأنّ المحبّ لله
تعالى يحبّ الله تعالى عند النعم وعند فقدها وعلى كل حال
حبّا صحيحا منعه أو أعطاه أو ابتلاه أو عافاه فالمحبّة لازمة
لقلبه على حالة واحدة فى العقد ثمّ هى الى الزيادة أقرب ،
ولو كانت على قدر النعم لنقصت المحبّة اذا نقصت النعم
فى وقت الشدائد ووقوع البلاء لكن المحبّ لله تعالى الذى
وله عقله بربّه واشتغل برضاه فكان فى شكره لله وذكره
له والتجرى لله برضايه

خيرنا كأنه ليست نعمة على احد إلّا وهي عليه وهو مشغول
بحبّه لله عزّ وجلّ عن كل الخلق وقد اسقطت المحبّة لله
تعالى عن قلبه الكبر والغلّ والحسد والبغي وكثيرًا ممّا
يعنيه من أمر الدنيا من مصلحة فكيف يذكر ما لا يعنيه،
قال بعض الحكماء من أعطي من المحبّة شيئًا فلم يُعطَ مثله
من الخشية فهو مخدوع، وروى عن الفضيل بن عياض
رحمه الله أنه قال الحبّ أفضل من الخوف ، (قال) وحدّثنا
اسمعيل بن محمّد قال حدّثني زهير البصري قال لقيت
شعوانة فقالت لي ما أحسن طريقتك إلّا أنك تنكر المحبّة
(قال) قلت ما أنكرها (قال) فقالت لي أتحبّ ربّك فقلت
نعم قالت فكيف تخاف ألّا يحبّك وأنت تحبّه قلت أنا أحبّه
لما أولاني وما اندأني من معرفته ونعمه (×) ولي ذنوب أخاف
أن لا يحبّني لما اكسبت نغشى عليها ثمّ أفاقت فقالت نه ،
قال أبو سعيد رحمه الله تعالى ما أحسن ما قال هذا الرجل
هذا كلام صحيح

قال أبو سعيد قدّس الله روحه قال رجل من رؤساء
البدلاء من يحبّ الله كثيرًا الشأن فيمن يحبّه الله ، وبالله
له وكثير له شيء له يعطى

التوفيق وفى هذا بلاغ لمن أعانه الله تعالى وسدّده وما بقى من صفات المحبّين أكثر

باب ثمّ الصدق فى الرضاعن الله عزّوجلّ، قال الله عزّ وجلّ فَلَا وَرَبِّكَ لَا يُؤْمِنُونَ حَتَّى يُحَكِّمُوكَ فِيمَا شَجَرَ بَيْنَهُمْ ثُمَّ لَا يَجِدُوا فِى أَنْفُسِهِمْ حَرَجًا مِمَّا قَضَيْتَ وَيُسَلِّمُوا تَسْلِيمًا، قال بعض العلماء رحمهم الله تعالى ماشهد الله تعالى لهم بالايمان حين لم يرضوا بحكم نبيّه فكيف اذا لم يرضوا بحكمه عزّوجلّ، قلت فما علامة الرضا فى القلب و ما موجوده قال سرورا القلب بمرّ القضاء، وقال بعضهم الرضا تلقّى المصائب بالرجاء والبشر، وروى عن أنس بن مالك رضى الله عنه أنّه قال كنت خادم النبى صلّى الله عليه وسلّم فما قال لى لشئ قطّ لم فعلت أوألا فعلت انّما كان يقول كذا قضى وكذا قدّر، وروى عن عمر بن الخطّاب رضى الله عنه أنه قال ما أبالى على ما أصبحتُ وما أمسيت على ما أحبّ أوعلى ما أكره لأنّى لا أدرى أيهما خيرلى، وقال عمر أيضا والرّب الصبر والشكر بعيران لى ما أبالى على أيهما ركبت، فهذا يدلّك على الرضا من قول عمر رضى الله عنه لأنّ الصبر لا يكون إلّا

له وجوده ﴿ ناقص فى الاصل ﴿ وكذى ﴿ صبحت

على ما يكره والشكر لا يكون إلّا على ما يحبّ فقال لا أبالى
أيّهما وقع لى وذلك لاستواء الحالين عنده، ويروى عن
عبد الله بن مسعود رضى الله عنه أنّه قال حبّذا المكروهان
وأيم الله ما هوا إلّا الغنى والفقر وإن حقّ كلّ واحد منهما
لواجب إن كان الغنى أنّ فيه العطف وإن كان الفقر أنّ
فيه الصبر، (٢١) وقال عمر بن عبد العزيز رضى الله عنه
أصبحت ومالى فى الأمور من اختيار، وقال بعضهم ومالى من
النعم سوى مواقع القدر قّ كائنا ما كان، (قال) وكان قد سقى
السمّ فقيل له تعالج فقال أنّ شفائى فى أن أمّ أمس أنفى
أو أذنى ما فعلت، وقال النبى صلّى الله عليه وسلّم لابن مسعود
رضى الله عنه يا بن أمّ عبد لا يكبرنّ همّك ما يقدّرنّ كن وما
ترزق تأكله، وقال النبى صلّى الله عليه وسلّم فى قصّة
طويلة لابن عبّاس رضى الله عنهما فإن استطعت أن تعمل لله
بالرضا فى اليقين وإلّا فنى الصبر على ما تكره خير كبير، أفلا ترى
أنّه صلّى الله عليه وسلّم دعاه الى أعلى الحالين، وقال بعض
الحكماء اذا استتمّ فى العبد الزهد والتوكّل والمحبّة واليقين
والحياء صحّ له الرضا، وهو عندنا كما قال وإلّا فهو مع الناس

أوقات وخطرات على قدر ايمانهم ثمّ يعودون الى الصبر،
وقال بعضهم الرضا قليل ومعوّل المؤمن الصبر

فقلت اشرح لي قول الحكيم الراضى يتلقّى المصائب بالبشر
والسرور وقال إنّ العبد لما صدق فى محبّته وقعت بينه وبين
الله تعالى المفاوضة والتسليم فزالت عن قلبه التهم وسكن
الى حسن اختيار من أحبّه ونزل فى حسن تدبيره وذاق طعـم
الوجود به فامتلأ قلبه فرحا ونعيما وسرورا فغلب ذلك ألم
المصائب والمكروه والبلوى فصار اسم البلوى عليه معلّقًا
فيستخرج منه اذا نزل به أمور كبيرة فتارة يتنعّم بعلمه
به اذا علم أنه يراه فى البلوى وتارة يعلم أنه ذكره فابتلاه
ولم يغفل عنه على عظيّم قدره أن يولّى من أمره مافيه الصلاح
فيراه تارة يشكو اليه شكوى المحبّ الى حبيبه وتارة يأتّ
اليه وتارة يطمع أن يراه راضيا عنه، فهكذا قال (*) جلّ ذكره
يَا أَيَّتُهَا ٱلنَّفْسُ ٱلْمُطْمَئِنَّةُ ٱرْجِعِى إِلَىٰ رَبِّكِ رَاضِيَةً مَّرْضِيَّةً،
فالرضا تعجّله العقلاء عن الله عزّ وجلّ فى الدنيا قبل الأخرة
فخرجوا من الرضا الى الرضا، وهكذا قال عزّ وجلّ رَضِىَ ٱللَّهُ
عَنْهُمْ وَرَضُوا عَنْهُ وَأَعَدَّ لَهُمْ جَنَّاتٍ الآية، فقد ذكرنا بعض

له معلق له عظم

صفات الراضين من ظاهر ما أمكن أن يذكر مثله فى كتاب و
ما بقى من صفاتهم أكثر وبالله التوفيق

باب ثمّ الصدق فى الشوق الى الله عزّ وجلّ ، روى عن
النبى صلّى الله عليه وسلّم أنه كان يقول فى دعائه اللهمّ
إنّى أسألك لذّة العيش بعد الموت والنظر الى وجهك و
الشوق الى لقائك ، وروى عن أبى الدرداء رضى الله عنه أنه
كان يقول أحبّ الموت اشتياقا الى ربّى ، وروى عن حذيفة
رضى الله عنه أنه قال عند الموت حبيب جاء على فاقة لا
أفلح من ندم ، وروى عن شهر بن حوشب رضى الله عنه
أنه قال أخذت معاذ رضى الله عنه قرحة فى حلقه فقال
اخنق خنقك فوعزّتك إنّى أحبّك ، (قال) وكان على بن سهل
المدائنى رحمه الله يقوم اذا هدأت العيون فينادى بصوت
له محزون يا من اشتغلت قلوب خلقه عنه بما يعقبهم عند
لقائه ندا و يا من سهت قلوب عباده عن الاشتياق اليه اذ
كانت أياديه اليهم قبل معرفتهم به ثمّ يبكى حتى تبكى
لبكائه جيرته ثمّ ينادى ليت شعرى سيّدى الى متى تحبسنى
ابعثنى سيّدى الى حسن وعدك وأنت العليم أنّ الشوق
لك المدنى

قد برّح بى وطال على الانتظار ثمّ يخرّ مغشيا عليه فلا يزال
كذلك حتى يحرك لصلاة الصبح، (قال) وكان الحارث بن
عمير رحمه الله يقول اذا أصبحت ونفسى وقلبى مصرّ
على حبّك سيّدى ومشتاق الى لقائك فعجّل بذلك قبل أن
يأتينى سواد الليل فاذا أمسى قال مثل ذلك فلم يزل على
مثل هذا الحال ستين سنة (٢٢) فالمشتاق الى الله تعالى
هو المتبرّم بالدنيا والبقاء فيها وهو محبّ للموت وانقضاء
المدّة والأجل، ومن علامته التوحّش من الخلق ولزوم
العزلة والانفراد بالوحدة ومن شأنه القلق والحنين و
الحزن والنحيب والكمد والغصّة المنكسرة فى الصدر
بشدّة الشّغف والكلف والهذيان بذكر المحبوب والارتياح
اليه والفكرة الصافية بهيجان الهمّة وجولان الروح فى
الغيوب لطلب اللقاء والبهت والدهش والحيرة عند توهّم
الظفر بالأمل من المأمول ونسيان حظّه من الدنيا والآخرة
إلّا رؤية من هو اليه مشتاق نعم ثمّ يعارضه الآن الخوف
الذى هو الخوف أنه لا يصل الى محبوبه ويخاف أن يقطع
به دونه ويحال بينه وبينه ويحجب عنه ثمّ يخاف أن

تحدث حادثة اذكان فى دارالبلوى فقد طالت عليه الأيّام
والليالى الى أن يخرج من الدنيا سالما على الامرالذى يرضى
مولاه ، فهذا بعض مايمكن ذكرُه من صفات المشتاقين و
مابقى من نعتهم أكثر وبالله التوفيق

باب ثمّ الصدق فى الأنس بالله تعالى وبذكره وقربه،
قال بعض الحكماء الانسُ بالله جلّ ثناؤه أُرقّ وأعذب من
الشوق لأنّ المشتاق كان بينه وبين الله تعالى مسافة
خفيفة لعلّة شوقه والمستأنس أقرب من الله عزّ وجلّ،
وهكذا روى عن النبى صلّى الله عليه وسلّم حين أتاه جبريل
عليه السلام فى صورة رجل فسأله عن الاسلام والايمان ثمّ
سأله عن الاحسان فقال له النبى صلّى الله عليه وسلّم تعبد
الله كأنّك تراه فإن لم تكن تراه فإنّه يراك فقال له صدقت،
وروى عن النبى صلّى الله عليه وسلّم أنّه قال لابن عمر
رضى الله عنه اعبد الله كأنّك تراه فإن لم تكن تراه فإنّه
يراك، (٭) واتّمادلّه على قرب الله عزّ وجلّ وقيامه عليه،
ومن قرب الله تعالى تستخرج حقائق الامور فى كلّ مقام،
فمن كان مقامه الخوف أدركه من قرب الله تعالى حين علم

ه ناقص فى الاصل ىه والانس

أنه يراه الحذر والفرق والخشية، ومن كان مقامه المحبّة أدركه من حقائق قرب الله تعالى حين علم أنه يراه الفرح و السرور والنعيم والمسارعة في طلب رضاه والقربة ليراه منافسا راغبا يريد القربة اليه والمبالغة في محبّته، والصابر في وقت بلواه ومصيبته وما يتحمّله لسيّده ممّا يقرّبه من ثوابه حين سمع الله عزّ وجلّ يقول إِنَّ ٱللَّهَ مَعَ ٱلصَّابِرِينَ وقال تعالى وَٱصْبِرْ لِحُكْمِ رَبِّكَ فَإِنَّكَ بِأَعْيُنِنَا سهل عليه عند ذلك معالجة الصبر واحتمال مؤنته، وكذلك أهل كل مقام عبد والله تعالى على القربة وذلك حين أيقنوا وهم الذين لا يكادون يصلون ولا يرجعون، وأمّا العامّة من الناس فإنّهم عملوا على ما انتهى اليهم من الامر والنهى على رجاء ضعيف فخلطوا ولم يحقّقوا

فمن صدق الانس ما يروى عن عروة بن الزبير رحمة الله عليه أنه خطب الى عبد الله بن عمر رضى الله عنهما ابنته وهو يطوف ببيت الله الحرام فلم يجبه ابن عمر ولم يردّ عليه جوابا ثمّ لقيه عبد الله بعد ذلك فقال له إنّك كلّمتنى فى الطواف ونحن نتخيّل الله بين أعيننا، فالمستأنس كأنّه له نتخايل

ينظر الى ما اشتاق اليه المشتاق، ويروى عن عبد الواحد بن
زيد البصرى رحمه الله تعالى أنه قال لأبى عاصم الشامى رضى
الله عنه ورحمه أما تشتاق الى الله تعالى قال لا انّما تشتاق
الى غائب فاذا كان الغائب شاهداً فالى من تشتاق فقال عبد
الواحد سقط الشوق، وروى عن داود الطائى رحمه الله تعالى
وكان من أئمّة المسلمين (٢٣) الذين أجمعوا على صدقه
وعدالته قال أيضا انّما تشتاق الغائب، قال بعض العلماء
رحمه الله وانّما قالوا هذا من حقائق الوجود لقرب الله عزّ
وجلّ معه اذكان معهم شاهد لا يغيب وذلك من الله
تعالى تسكين وتطمين ورحمة وراحة عجّلها لهم فى الدنيا
والّا فما الذى وصل اليهم من الله عزّ وجلّ من قربة
فمن علامة المستأنس بالله تعالى وبقربه أن يكون
واجداً لذكر الله عزّ وجلّ فى قلبه واجداً لقربه منه لا يفقده
على كل حال وفى كل وقت وكل موطن ويكون الله عزّ وجلّ
وقربه السابق اليه قبل الاشياء وذلك اذا اسكن قلبه نور
قرب الله تعالى منه فيه ينظر الى الاشياء وبه يستدلّ على
الاشياء، وهكذا يروى عن عامر بن عبد الله رضى الله عنه

أنه قال ما نظرت الى شئ قط إلا كان الله تعالى أقرب الىّ
منه ، ومن صفات المستأنس أن يكون متبرّما بالأهل و
الخليقة كلّهم مستعذ بالخلوة والوحدة ويكون في البيت
المظلم متبرّما بالمصباح اذا راه بل يجيف بابه ويسبل ستره
ويواحد قلبه ويألف قرب مليكه فيكون به أنيسا وبمناجاته
متنعّما ويكون متفرّغا من طارق يطرقه فينقص عليه
خلوته نعم ثمّ تراه مستوحشا من ضوء الشمس اذا دخل
عليه في صلاته ويتثاقل تلقاء الخلق ويملّهم ويكون
لقاؤهم ومجالستهم عليه غراما وخسارا فاذا جنّته الليل
ونامت العيون وهدأت الحركات وسكنت حواسّ الاشياء
خلا عند ذلك ببثّه فهاج شجوه وتصاعدت أنفاسه وطال
أنينه وتنجّزا الموعود من مأموله وما قد غذاه من فوائده
وألطافه فظفر عند ذلك ببعض سوله وقضى بعض أوطاره
(٭) وكذلك المستأنس تذهب عنه الوحشة في المواطن
التى يفزع فيها الناس فيستوى عنده العمران والخراب و
القفار والجماعة والوحدة وذلك للذى استولى عليه من
قرب الله عزّ وجلّ وعذوبة ذكره ويغلب ما سواه من العوارض

له وهدت

الظاهرة والباطنة، فهذا ظاهر الانس الذى يمكن أن يذكر
وما بقى من مقامات الانس أكثر وأعزم من أن يكون فى كتاب
إلّا أن يجرى منه شئ عند المذاكرة مع أهله وبالله التوفيق
واعلم أيها السائل عن الصدق وشرحه أن الذى ذكرته
لك انّما هو ظاهر الصدق والصبر والاخلاص الذى لا يسع
الناس جهله ولا ترك العمل به خاصّة المريدين من الناس
الطالبين لسلوك سبيل النجاة ومن الناس من لا يكون له
عند الله تعالى إلّا هذا العلم الظاهر والعمل الظاهر فيعمل
فى ذلك ويصدق فيه فيؤديه ذلك الى رحمة الله تعالى و
ثوابه وله عند الله خير كثير، ومن الناس من يصدق فى
هذه المقامات التى ذكرناها وأكثر فيؤديه ذلك فى
عاجل الدنيا الى المقام الرفيع والعلم بالله والمقام الشريف
فيصير الى الروح والراحة والنعمة بمعرفة الله عزّ وجلّ و
الظفر بقرب الله تعالى والوصول الى المنزلة الشريفة التى
يدق وصفها وشرحها، وقال بعض العلماء بالله تعالى إنّ
الله يكرم أولياءه بكرامة لا يطلع عليها العباد لا فى الدنيا
ولا فى الآخرة، ألم تسمع لقول الله عزّ وجلّ فَلَا تَعْلَمُ نَفْسٌ

مَا أُخْفِيَ لَهُم مِّن قُرَّةِ أَعْيُنٍ ، ويقال فى الحديث فيعطون ما
لا عين رأت ولا أذن سمعت ولا خطر على قلب بشر، وهكذا
كل قوم على أقدارهم ، ومنهم من لا تنقضى كرامته من ثواب
الله تعالى ومن النعيم فى الجنان ومنهم من لا تنقضى كرامته
من الله تعالى (٢٤) والزيادة من برّه والنظر اليه ، وقد صحّ
الخبر عن النبى صلّى الله عليه وسلّم أنه قال إنّ أدنى أهل
الجنّة منزلة من ينظر فى ملكه ألفى عام يرى أقصاه كما
يرى أدناه ، ومنهم من ينظر الى وجه الله جلّ وعزّ كلّ يوم
مرّتين ، ومحال أن يكونوا هؤلاء سواء وكان علمهم فى الدنيا
سواء ، قال جلّ ذكره وَلَقَدْ فَضَّلْنَا بَعْضَ ٱلنَّبِيِّينَ عَلَىٰ
بَعْضٍ فلم يقع التفضّل على الخلق إلّا بفضل علمهم بالله
تعالى والمعرفة به ثمّ على قدر هذا الأناس تفاوتوا فى
الدنيا والآخرة وبالله التوفيق

قلت فهل يصيّر العبد الى حال يفقد مطالبة الصدق
من نفسه ويسقط عنه مؤنة الاعمال وأثقال الاخلاص
ومؤنة الصبر ويكون عاملا بالصدق فأخذ ممّا ذكرت
وأكثر بلا اشتغال ولا تعب قال نعم ألم تسمع الحديث
لله يصر له فاجا

الذى يروى ان الجنّة حفّت بالمكاره وحفّت النار بالشهوات،
ويروى فى خبر آخر ان الحقّ ثقيل مرىّ وان الباطل خفيف
وبئ، والنفس مجبولة بحبّ هذه الدار والسكون اليها
وحبّ الدعة والراحة فيها والحقّ واتّباعه والعمل به و
الصدق وأخلاقه نذلك كلّه هو خلاف محبوب النفس فاذا
عقل العبد عن الله تعالى وفهم ما دعاه اليه من العزوف عن هذه
الدّار الفانية والرغبة فى الدار الباقية حمل عند ذلك
نفسه على احتمال المكاره من ركوب طريق الصدق وعزم
على بذل المجهود وصبر لله تعالى وكابد نفسه واستعان
بالله تعالى فنظر الله تعالى اليه راغبا فيما لديه حريصا
على أن يرضيه وعاد عليه عند ذلك بلطفه وعونه فسهّل
عليه العسير ممّا استصعب من نفسه وأبدله بالمرارة
حلاوة وبالثقل خفّة وبالخشونة لينا ودعة (٭) فسهل
عليه قيام الليل وصارت المناجاة لله تعالى والخلوة بخدمته
له نعيما بعد شدّة المكابدة وصار الصيام والظمأ فى
الهواجر خفيفا عليه حين ذاق عذوبة مارجا من روح الله
تعالى وحسن عاقبته وكذلك تبدّلت وسهلت الاخلاق والاحوال
له عاد

عليه حين قام له من كل مقام عاناه وكابده لله تعالى التماس
رضاه عوضا مكانه من الخير فتغيّرت عند ذلك أخلاقه و
انتقل طبعه وهدأت نفسه وانتعش عقله وسكنه نور
الحقّ فألفه ونفرعنه الهوى وطفئت ظلمته فصار عند
ذلك الصدق وأخلاقه طبعا له لا يحسّن غيره ولا يألف إلّا
ايّاه ولا يسكّن الى غيره واكتنفته العصمة من ربّه فضعف
عند ذلك كيد عدقّه وصار مغلوبا حين ماتت دواعيه من
الباطل وكلّ سلاحه بموت الهوى وانقياد النفس حين
تخلّقت بأخلاق المرحومين ، قال الله جلّ ذكره حين أخبر
عن يوسف عليه السلام إِنَّ ٱلنَّفْسَ لَأَمَّارَةٌ بِٱلسُّوٓءِ إِلَّا
مَا رَحِمَ رَبِّي ، فأ نفس الانبياء والصدّ يقين عليهم السّلام
مرحومة معصومة وكذلك كل مؤمن على حسب قوّة ايمانه
فسقطت عند ذلك عن العبد معاناة الصدق وثقل العمل
به فصار عاملا بالصدق الذى ذكرناه وأكثر بأضعاف كثيرة
بلا مؤنة بل صار ذلك نعيما وغذاء إن تركه توحّش من
وتفزّع من فقده فصار الصدق وأخلاقه صفة له لا يحسن
غيرها حتى كأنه لم يزل، كذلك ومصداق ذلك فى الكتاب
له وهدت له تحسن له تالف له تسكن له معاية

والسّنة موجود قال الله تعالى وَالَّذِينَ جَاهَدُوا فِينَا لَنَهْدِيَنَّهُمْ سُبُلَنَا وَإِنَّ اللَّهَ لَمَعَ الْمُحْسِنِينَ وقال عزّ وجلّ وَعَدَ اللَّهُ الَّذِينَ آمَنُوا مِنكُمْ وَعَمِلُوا الصَّالِحَاتِ (٢٥) لَيَسْتَخْلِفَنَّهُمْ فِي الْأَرْضِ كَمَا اسْتَخْلَفَ الَّذِينَ مِن قَبْلِهِمْ وَلَيُمَكِّنَنَّ لَهُمْ دِينَهُمُ الَّذِي ارْتَضَى لَهُمْ وَلَيُبَدِّلَنَّهُم مِّن بَعْدِ خَوْفِهِمْ أَمْنًا يَعْبُدُونَنِي لَا يُشْرِكُونَ بِي شَيْئًا وقال عزّ وجلّ وَنُرِيدُ أَن نَّمُنَّ عَلَى الَّذِينَ اسْتُضْعِفُوا فِي الْأَرْضِ وَ نَجْعَلَهُمْ أَئِمَّةً وَنَجْعَلَهُمُ الْوَارِثِينَ وَنُمَكِّنَ لَهُمْ فِي الْأَرْضِ وقال عزّ من قائل وَجَعَلْنَا مِنْهُمْ أَئِمَّةً يَهْدُونَ بِأَمْرِنَا لَمَّا صَبَرُوا عن الدنيا وإنما أردنا أن نثبت المجاهدة للنفوس و بذل الجهد فى الصدق ثمّ ان المعونة من الله تأتى من بعد ذلك والحجّة فى ذلك قائمة فى السنن، قال ابن عبّاس رضى الله عنهما فى تفسير سورة طه قال معنى طه يا رجل بلسان الحبشية مَا أَنزَلْنَا عَلَيْكَ الْقُرْآنَ لِتَشْقَى قال لتعنى به، أفلا ترى أنه حين قام صلّى الله عليه وسلّم لله عزّ وجلّ شكرا حتى تورّمت قد ماه شكر لله تعالى فأمره بالهدوّ، وقد روى أن النبى صلّى الله عليه وسلّم كان

 له ناقص فى الاصل له ولا

يتعبّد فى جبل حراء الشهر وأكثر وكذلك يروى أن النبى صلّى
الله عليه وسلّم كان يحرس ويحفظ من عدوّه حتى نزلت هذه
الآية وَاللّٰهُ يَعْصِمُكَ مِنَ النَّاسِ فنحّى الحرس تصديقا لقول
الله عزّ وجلّ حين ذكره له أنه يعصمه فأيقن وسكن صلّى
الله عليه وسلّم وكذلك المؤمنون يأتيهم اليقين بعد الضعف،
وكذلك النبى صلّى الله عليه وسلّم كان يخرج الى الغار بالجبل
الذى يقال له ثور ويختبى هو وأبو بكر الصديق رضى الله
عنه ثمّ يخرجان الى المدينة هاربين فى السرّ وهذا انّما كان
وقت البلوى من الله تعالى له اذ كان له عليه السلام فى مقام
الصبر والمجاهدة ثمّ من بعد ما صار الى المدينة عليه
السلام تغزوه قريش يوم وقعة أحد تقتل أصحابه وتكسر
رباعيّته عليه السلام وتدمّى وجهه ، أفلا ترى انّ الهوى
(✱) والمحنة لازمة له وللمؤمنين طالبة لهم، ثمّ إنّه
صلّى الله عليه وسلّم يخرج هو وأصحابه فيهلّ ويسوق
الهدى يريد العمرة فتمنعه قريش من دخول مكّة حتى
اضطرب النّاس فأحلّ بالموضع الذى يسمّى الحديبية ورجع
ولم يدخل الحرم، ثمّ انظر الآن حين انقضت مدّة البلاء و
له ننجّا له ويدما

جاء النصر كيف دخل مكة صلى الله عليه وسلم فقتل و
أمّن من شاء ثمّ نشر عندها بالمغفرة فأنزل الله عزّ وجلّ
إِنَّا فَتَحْنَا لَكَ فَتْحًا مُبِينًا لِيَغْفِرَ لَكَ ٱللهُ مَا تَقَدَّمَ مِنْ
ذَنْبِكَ وَمَا تَأَخَّرَ الآية

وهذا موسى صلى الله عليه وسلم ومنزلته عند الله
فانظر الى عظيم بلائه حين حملت به أمّه كيف ذبحت
النساء وقتل الولدان فى طلب موسى عليه السلام فرجع
بلاؤه على الخليقة ثمّ أخبر الله عزّ وجلّ عنه فقال فَأَصْبَحَ
فِى ٱلْمَدِينَةِ خَائِفًا يَتَرَقَّبُ وقال إِنَّ ٱلْمَلَأَ يَأْتَمِرُونَ
بِكَ لِيَقْتُلُوكَ فَٱخْرُجْ إِنِّى لَكَ مِنَ ٱلنَّاصِحِينَ فَخَرَجَ مِنْهَا
خَائِفًا يَتَرَقَّبُ قَالَ رَبِّ نَجِّنِى مِنَ ٱلْقَوْمِ ٱلظَّالِمِينَ، ثمّ
انظر أيّها المريد الطالب للوصول الى كرامة الله عزّ وجلّ
بالتوانى والتفريط ألم يبلغك أنّ موسى عليه السلام لم
يصل الى امرأته حتى رعى الغنم وخدم عشر سنين ثمّ أرسل
الله تعالى وكلّمه وأظهر برهانه فقال لَا تَخَافَا إِنَّنِى
مَعَكُمَا أَسْمَعُ وَأَرَى فحين قال لهما لَا تَخَافَا هل خافا
ألم يجعل لهما آية فى عصّا نظهرا على كيد السحرة وهزما
به الله لك به الوصول به عصى

الجيوش ثمّ أداله الله تعالى من أعدائه وأغرقهم أجمعين
وهذا يوسف عليه السلام حين أخبر الله تعالى عنه أنه
يلقى فى الجبّ ثمّ يباع بثمن بخس دراهم معدودة وكانوا
فيه من الزَّاهِدِينَ ثمّ لم يفارقه البلاء حتى فتن بامرأة
العزيز وسجن السنين الكثيرة، ثمّ انظر كيف أداله الله
تعالى (٢٦) على أخوته ثمّ أخرجهم الله تعالى فأظهر برهانه
وجعله على خزائن الأرض، وكذلك الانبياء الذّين ذكرهم
الله عزّ وجلّ عليهم السلام وفى هذا بلاغ لمن فهم عن الله
عزّ وجلّ وعن العلماء الادلّاء على الطريق الى الله عزّ وجلّ
وهذا عمر بن الخطّاب رضى الله عنه وما روى عنه
أنه ما سلك طريقا قط إلّا سلك الشيطان طريقا غيرها و
قال إنّ الشيطان ليفرّ من جبين عمر وقد كان بالامس من
اللات والعزى فى امور ترضى الشيطان، فانظر كيف أخلص
لله تعالى وصدّق إن كان منه العدوّ وباطله، وروى عن
ثابت البنانى رحمة الله عليه أنه قال كابدت القرآن
عشرين سنة وتنعمت به عشرين سنة، وقال بعض الحكماء
إنّ القوم لم يزالوا يمضون الصبر حتى صار عسلا، وقال بعض
له البلى له الذى له يمضوا

الحكماء إنّ دون كل بِرّ عقبة فمن تجشّم ركوبها أفضت به
الى الراحة ومن هاله ركوب العقبة فلم يرقها بقى مكانه
قلت فلا بدّ من هذا البلوى والاختبار قال لا بدّ منه لكلّ
عبد رفيع القدر عند الله عزّ وجلّ من اهل المعرفة بالله عزّ
وجلّ، وقد صحّ الخبر عن النبى صلّى الله عليه وسلّم أنه سئل
من أشدّ الناس بلاء قال الانبياء ثمّ الصالحون ثمّ الامثل
فالامثل، يبتلى العبد على حسب دينه فإن كان فى ايمانه قوّة
شدّد عنيه البلاء وإن كان فى ايمانه ضعف خفّف عليه
البلاء فالانبياء عليهم السلام بادأهم الحقّ عزّ وجلّ بكرامة
الرسالة وبشّرهم بالنبوّة ثمّ حمل عليهم البلاء فاحتملوا
البلاء بقدر الكرامة التى أكرمهم بها حتى راضهم بالبلاء
وتفقّهوا فيه وبه صبروا لله عزّ وجلّ حتى نصروا، والمؤمنو
قامت لهم الرغبة فى ثواب الله عزّ وجلّ الذى وعدهم و
الرهبة من عقابه الذى به تواعدهم فصبروا لله تعالى و
أخلصوا وصدقوا فشكرا لله تعالى لهم ذلك وأظهر برهانهم
على الخليقة فجعلهم علماء يقتدى بهم وأسكن اليقين
قلوبهم، (٭) ثمّ إنّ المؤمنين بعد ذلك على وجهين،

ـ ناقص فى الاصل كله البلى ڪ البلى

فمنهم من يبدأه الله تعالى بالنعمة والمنّة والموهبة فيهب
له الانابة ويحبّب اليه البرّ ويسهّل عليه الطاعة ويبدأ
بالمنن الكثيرة فاذا تمكّن الروح فى قلبه واستعان بالأعمال
الصالحة حمل عليه بعد ذلك البلاء والاختبار والمصائب
والضرّاء والعسر والشدّة نعم ثمّ توجد منه الحلاوة التى
كان يجدها والنشاط فى البرّ ثقل عليه الطاعة بعد خفّتها
ويجد المرارة بعد الحلاوة والكسل بعد النشاط والكدر
بعد الصفاء رذلك لعلّة البلوى والاختبار فتعتريه الفترة،
فإن جاهد الآن وصبر واحتمل المكروه صار الى حدّ الراحة
والبلوغ وأضعف له البرّ ظاهرا وباطنا، وهكذا يروى
فى الحديث إنّ لكلّ شرّة فترة فمن كانت فترته الى سنّة
فقد نجا ومن كانت فترته الى بدعة فقد هلك، وقال أبو بكر
الصدّيق رضى الله عنه طوبى لمن مات فى النأمة بدو
الاسلام وشرّته، ويروى فى الحديث ان الله عزّ وجلّ
يأمر جبريل عليه السلام فيقول اقبض حلاوة الطاعة من
قلب عبدى فإن تأسّف عليها فردّها عليه وزده وإلّا فدعه،
ويروى فى حديث أخر ان الله عزّ وجلّ يقول إن أدنى ما اصنع

بالعالم اذا ركن الى الدنيا أن أنزع حلاوة مناجاته ايّاى

من صدره وأن أدعه فى الدنيا حيرانا، وفى خبر أخر أن العبد

اذا ركن الى الدنيا بعد العلم والمعرفة والعلم بالبصيرة يقول

الله عزّ وجلّ لجبريل عليه السلام انزع حلاوة مناجاته ايّاى

من صدره وأعطه من الدنيا مقصما يشتغل به عنّى، وأما

العبد الثانى فإنه يبدأ بالصدق والاعمال الصالحـة و

أخلاق الصدق ثمّ يعمل فى ذلك ما شاء الله عزّ وجلّ فتأتيه

الكرامة بعد ذلك فيعطيه الله تعالى ما لم يرجّه ويحتسبه

(٢٧) وهكذا عامّة البدلاء لا تأتيهم الأيات والكرامات

إلّا من بعد العمل وبذل الجهد وأكثر ما لم يحتسبوا ما

أتاهم الله تعالى به حين بدأهم الله عزّ وجلّ به، ومنهم

من اطّلع على القوم وقيل له إنّك منهم فعمل بعد أن أخبر

بذلك، ومنهم من يعرف نفسه ولا يعرف غيره، ومنهم

من يعرف الجميع بأسمائهم وقبائلهم

فإن كنت أيها السائل عن الصدق وشرح الطريق

قد عملت فى الصدق ما ذكرته لك من العلم وباشرت هذه

المنازل ونزلت هذه المراحل وقطعت هذه الاسباب التى

له الصالحات له يرجوه له صدق

ذكرناها فأفضيت منها الى الراحة والسكون والاطمأنينة فأنت محاط بالعصمة وماض على سبيل الاستقامة والحجّة البيضاء التى توردك على الله عزّوجلّ فهنيئًا لك وبارك الله فيك فأنت من أمرك على بصيرة ، وإن كنت قد باشرت الصدق وعملت فى كل مقام البرّ بقدر طاقتك وما أذن الله تعالى لك وعاينت الامور فعسى أن يكون الله قد دراك وقد أبليت فيما بينك وبينه عذرًا لرغبتك فى التقرّب اليه فصحّ اليه افتقارك حين علمت أنه لا بدّ لك منه فألقيت كنفك بين يديه فعسى أن يكون قد دراك فى بعض الاوقات اليه قاصدًا راغبًا بنيّة صحيحة وعزم صادق علم أنك لا تملّ ولا تبرح من التعرّض له دون بلوغ مناك فجاد لك ببرّه وأعطاك بعض الامل منه بل جذب قلبك اليه جذبة فأسكنه اليقين وأشرف به على الآخرة فسهل عليك عند ذلك العسير وألان لك من نفسك الصعب الذ لول ثمّ اختصر بك الطريق اليه فقرّ قرارك وقامت حياتك و طاب عيشك فبذلك تعرّف السيّد الكريم الذى لا تنقصه المواهب ولا ينفد نائله لأنّه البرّ الرحيم الذى

تسمّى الشكور (*) فيا عجبا كل عجب وعجب كل متعجّب
ولا عجب اذ كان السّيد الكريم يفعل ما يريد ولكن موضع
العجب يلزم العبيد من شكره لعبيده الامر الذى بدأ هم به
ودلّهم عليه واستعملهم به وحفظ عليهم ثمّ أحبّهم عليه و
نسبه اليهم فعلا ثمّ كتبه لهم فى المقبول ثمّ أثنى به عليهم
بِمَ وعدهم عليه الجزاء فهذا البرّ الآن من الكريم لا تقف
عليه العباد بل تحيّر فيه العقول

هيهات أيها السائل المريد استيقظ من طول هـذ ه
الرقدة انّما هذه أسماء علقها عليهم أ نّهم فاعلون وامور
نسبها اليهم وما أظنّه إلّا له والتوفيق به والصنعة منه فى
صنعته التى تفرّد بإنشائها وإبداعها لمّا شاء وهو الفعّال
لما يريد الذى يصيب برحمته من يشاء ، والعقلاء عن الله
عزّ وجلّ من عباده يتلقّون الامور على هذا الوصف الشرح
ويرجعون فى الاشياء اليه ويرونها منه سبحانه لأنـه
كان بدوها وعليه تمامها فهو القائم بها واليه مرجعها
ولله الامر من قبل ومن بعد أَلَا لَهُ ٱلْخَلْقُ وَٱلْأَمْرُ
تَبَارَكَ ٱللَّهُ رَبُّ ٱلْعَالَمِينَ ، وأمّا الضعفاء من الخلق

له فاعلين

فإنّهم يرون لأنفسهم ها هنا فعلاً، هيهات اذا صدقوا و
أخلصوا طلبوا الجزاء من الله عزّ وجلّ على ذلك وذلك
مبلغهم من العلم ولهم عند الله تعالى خير كبير، (قال) و
أذكرلك مقاماً أخرى فأعرض نفسك وغيرك ممّن تراه
من العبيد يثير الى المعرفة والعلم والسكون الى الله عزّ وجلّ
فإن كنت قد شربت بكأس المعرفة بالله تعالى فأطلعك
الله بصفاء اليقين على ما سبق لك عنده فى القديم حين
أرادك قبل أن تريده وكان لك عالماً قبل أن تعرفه وذكرك
قبل أن تذكره وأحبّك قبل أن تحبّه فهاج منك الآن
الشكر له على أياديه فألزمت قلبك المحبّة على أياديه
فأثرته وارتاحت روحك اليه فألفت قربه فصرت الآن
اليه تأوى وفى قربه تسكن فهولا يغيب عنك ولا تفقده
ذاهباً وجائياً (٢٨) وقائماً وقاعداً ويقظاناً ورا قداً وعلى كل
حال، أما سمعت ما يذكر عن النبى صلّى الله عليه وسلم
حين يقول تنام عيناى ولا ينام قلبى، وكذلك المؤمنون على
أقدارهم، فما أعظم شأنك أيها العبد وأجلّ خطبك اذ
كان السيّد الكريم الكبير المتعالى الغنى الحميد ذكرك

سله المتعال

ذكرا بعد ذكر فخصّك فأجزل لك العطيّة اذ ذلك على حجّته
فأثرته فكان هو بغيتك ومرادك ومنتهى رغبتك وليس
منك شئ تملكه للعباد ولكنّها موهبة وهى أوّل أعلام
الوصول الى الراحة أن يكون الله مراد العباد لا غيره ، و
من علامة ذلك أن يكون هو الحافظ عليك ما استودع
قلبك من ذكره ومودّته وأوجد لك من قربه وتعطّف عليك
ببرّه فسامحك الآن فسقطت عنك حركات الطلب للظفر أو
التقرّب إلّا حركة تهيج منك الآن شكرا له على أياديه
وإيجابا لحقّه وألفة له على غيره والتنعّم بمناجاته ولذّة
خدمته وما أراد فيك من تعبّده بمشيئته ليريك موضع
قدرته واختلاف أحكامه عليك لتفقه عنه وأنت فى ذلك
واجد لقربه وغير متشاغل بحركاتك ولا طالب منه عليها
جزاء وثوابا كما أراد العباد والزهّاد ولكن تعمل لله تعالى
حبّا وكرما لأنه خلقك كرما واستعملت بأخلاق الكرماء
وبالله التوفيق

وهذا الآن جواب لك أخر على مسألتك حين قلت هل
يصير العبد الى حال يفقد مطالبة الصدق من نفسه وهى
له المرب له اوالفة له طالبا

علامة الواصلين فاعلمها، أما علمت أيتها المريد أن الورع
والزهد والصبر والتوكّل والخوف والرجاء والمراقبة والحياء
والمحبّة والشوق والأنس والصدق فى المواطن والاخلاص
فيها وكلّ خلق حسن جميل انّما هى منازل نزلها العمّال لله
عزّوجلّ (٭) ثمّ ارتحلوا منها الى غيرها حتى وصلوا الى المنى
من قرب سيّدهم، فما أنت وذكر المنزل الذى نزلته حتى
أوصلك الى بغيتك إن كنت واصلا ظافرا ببعض حظّك
من مطلوبك فأنت كأنّك مشاهده نعليه الآن فازدد إقبالا
واليه فأدم النظر وأصغ اليه بالأذان الواعية فإنه اقرب
اليك منك الى نفسك فما أنت الآن وذكر الصدق وانّما
هو منزل من منازل الطالبين

وبعد فإن كان قد فتح لك الباب الذى قد كان
بينك وبينه مغلقا وكشف عن قلبك الستر الذى كان
عليه مرخى فأوجدك قربه ولاطفك ببعض التأنّس نفسا ك
أن تكون قد صرت الى بعض سولك نقرّ قرارك ، وإن
كنت أنت وغيرك من الطالبين انّما فقدت وجود مطالبة
الصدق وما أشباهه من الامور من وجودك وجودك لقرب الله عزّ
له المنا

وجلّ والتشاغل به فتلك بغية العارفين بالله عزّ وجلّ و
كذلك فافهمها من نفسك ومن غيرك ولا تخدعنّ لنفسك
من حظّك من ربّك ، واعلم أنّ الواصلين الى الله عزّ وجلّ
وأهل القرب منه الذين قد ذاقوا طعم محبّة الله تعالى
بالحقيقة وظفروا بحظّهم من مليكهم فمن صفاتهم أنّ
الورع والزهد والصبر والاخلاص والصدق والتوكّل
والثقة والمحبّة والشوق والانس والاخلاق الجميلة وما
لم يمكن أن يوصف من أخلاقهم وما استوطنوه من البرّ و
الكرم فذلك كلّه معهم وساكنٌ في طبعهم ومخفيٌّ في
سرائرهم لا يحسنون غيره لأنه غذاؤهم وعادتهم لأنّهم
فرضوا ذلك على أنفسهم فرضا وعملوا فيه حتى ألفوه فلم
يكن عليهم بعد الوصول كلفة في اتيانه والعمل به اذا
حلّ وقت كلّ حال لأنّ ذلك غذاؤهم كما ليس لهم في اداء
الفرائض ثقل ولا علاج (۲۹) وذلك لما غلب على قلوبهم
من الأثرة لله عزّ وجلّ والقرب منه فهم عاملون به بلا مؤونة
بل بلا تشاغل بالاعمال الظاهرة لأنّ الخدمة والاعمال
الظاهرة انّما تقع على ظاهر الجوارح ، فانهم هذا الموضع
لله وساكنا لله ومخفا

والقلوب بعد ذلك ذاهلة بل هي بالله مشغولة للذى
استولى عليها من قرب الله عزّ وجلّ والمحبّة لله والشوق
اليه والرهبة منه والتعظيم له والاجلال ، فافهم أيها
المريد ما ألقيت اليك وتدبّره تجده بيّنا معروفا إن
شاء الله تعالى

فأحضر الآن عقلك واجمع همّك ولا تسمع العلم
وأنت عازب الفهم عن الذى يلقى اليك فلا عذر لك الآن
بعد العلم والبيان بل قد تأكّدت عليك الحجّة فاعمل
فى التخلّص الى الله عزّ وجلّ لعلّك أن تتخلّص فتقرّ عينك
بمعرفته فى هذه الدار عاجلا قبل الأجل، نعم ثمّ يدوم
حزنك ويشتدّ كربك وتزداد كل حال كنت تجدها أضعاف
ما كنت تجدها قبل المعرفة والوصول، ومصداق ذلك فى
كتاب الله عزّ وجلّ وسنّة نبيّه صلّى الله عليه وسلّم قال
الله عزّ وجلّ إِنَّمَا يَخْشَى ٱللَّهَ مِنْ عِبَادِهِ ٱلْعُلَمَاءُ وقال
النبى صلّى الله عليه وسلّم أنا أعلمكم بالله وأشدّكم
له خشية ، وقال صلّى الله عليه وسلّم لو تعلمون ما أعلم
لضحكتم قليلا ولبكيتم كثيرا ولخرجتم الى الصعدات

تجرُّون الى الله، وعلى حسب ذلك كان صلّى الله عليـه وسلّم، وكذلك العارف بالله القريب من الاشياء الموفّق فى كلّ حال يحلّ فيها بما يكون فيها بخلاف غيره من الناس، ثمّ على هذا القياس وفى هذا بلاغ لمن فهم وتدبّر وبالله التوفيق.

قلت متى يألف العبد أحكام مولاه ويسكن فى تدبيره واختياره قال الناس فى هذا على مقامين فافهم، فمن كان منهم اتّما يألف أحكام مولاه (ﷺ) ليقوم بأمره الذى يوصله الى ثوابه فذلك حسن وفيه خير كبير إلّا أنّ صاحبه يقوم ويقع ويصبر مرّة ويجزع أخرى ويرضى ويسخط ويعبر و يراجع الامر فذلك يؤديه الى ثواب الله ورحمته إلّا أنه معنّى فى شدّة ومكابدة وإنّما يألف العبد أحكام مولاه ويستعذب بلواه ويسكن فى حسن تدبيره واختياره بالكلّيّة بلا تلكّى من نفسه اذا كان العبد ألفا لمولاه ولذكره وهو له محبّ وادّ وبه راض وعنه راض، فهل يكون أيها السائل على المحبّ مؤونة فيما حكم عليه محبوبه كيف وإنّما يتلقّى ذلك بالسرور والنعيم هكذا قال فى الخبر حتى يعدّ البلاء له معنا

نعمة والرخاء مصيبة ، وقال فى خبر اخر غنيمة الصّدّيقين
ما زوى عنهم من الدّنيا ، وروى عن الله عزّ وجلّ فى بعض ما
أنزل من كتبه أنه قال معشر المتوجّهين الّى بحتّى ما
يضرّكم ما نا بكم من الدّنيا اذا كنت لكم حصنا وما يضرّكم
من عا داكم اذا كنت لكم سلما ، فمن كان مع الله عزّ و
جلّ بهذه الاحوال فى المواطن كيف يكون إلّا على نحو ما
ذكرناه ، ولقد قال بعض العلماء بالله تعالى واهل القرب
منه ان القوم الذى ذكرنا بعض أحوالهم لا يرضون من
أنفسهم أن تكون تقاوم الامور عند حلولها والاحداث
عند نوازلها حتى تتمكّن من قلوبهم فيحتاجون أن يصبروا
عليها أو يرضوا بها بل الصّبر والرضا لهم تابع مضاف لأنهم
طالبوا من أنفسهم صحّة الشغل بالله تعالى والانفراد به
فلم يرضوا عند ذلك أن تكون الامور النازلة بهم تقاوم
ذكر الله تعالى حتى تساويه وَٱللَّهُ غَالِبٌ عَلَىٰ أَمْرِهِ ، وبعد
فإنّهم عبيد محكوم عليهم وان أقلّ القليل فى الاوقات
ليملكهم حتّى يقرّون لله تعالى بالضعف (٣٠) ويسألونه
العون فلا تعجب ان بدا لك من أحد منهم شئ من ذلك فهذا
به تمكن

النبى صلّى الله عليه وسلّم يقول إنّى بشر اللهمّ من دعوت
عليه فاجعل دعائى عليه رحمة ، وسمعت بعض العلماء
بالله عزّ وجلّ يقول إن من شدّة اتّصال العبد بمولاه و
وجده به ونزوله فى قربه لا يجد طعم اختلاف الاحكام
بل يكون معه النظر الخفىّ اليها حتى كأنها على غيره أو
بغيره نازلة، فهذا غاية من التلقّى للاحكام فافهم هذا الوضع
وتدبّره فإنه يؤديك الى علم السكون الى الله عزّ وجلّ إن
شاء الله ، وانّما يكون السكون الى الله تعالى والاطمأنينة
على قدر القرب من القلب ، ومن شرح السكون الى الله تعا
فقد حسّ الاشياء من القلب وسكون دواعى الهمّ وهدوء
الضمير مع الله والى الله تعالى فعند ذلك تكون الامور من
الدنيا والآخرة وأعمال البرّ والطاعة طالبة للعبد ولاحقة
به واليه محتاجة واليه واصلة بل اليه موصولة لأنه
عزف عنها واستغنى بمالكها فوصلت اليه ، قال الله عزّ وجلّ
أَلَيْسَ اللَّهُ بِكَافٍ عَبْدَهُ ، وبلغنا أنّ الله عزّ وجلّ أوحى
الى عيسى عليه السلام أنزل لنى منك كهمّك واجعلنى ذخرا
لك فى معادك ، وروى عن النبى صلّى الله عليه وسلّم من
له موصول

غير طريق أنه قال من جعل الهمّ همّا واحدا كفاه الله سائر
همومه ، وروى عن الفضيل بن عياض رحمه الله أنّه قال
ما عجبت من عبادة ملك مقرّب ولا نبيّ مرسل اذ كان الله
عزّ وجلّ قوّاهم على ذلك ، وهكذا من ذكرناه من القوم و
صفاتهم فمن نظر الى عبيد الله تعالى بنفسه وقياسه و
بأنفسهم وما يشبههم فهم عنده فى موضع النقص أبدا
فاذا نظر اليهم بالله عزّ وجلّ وبقوّته وتدبيره فمّما يعجب
وبالله التوفيق (*)

مسئلة تدلّ على ما ذكرنا قلت فما تقول فى عبد
كان لا يتكلّم ولا يتحرّك ولا يعمل عملا إلّا طولب عليه
فى ذلك ووجد النقصان ولحقته الفترة والقسوة فى أوقات
نيله وأكله وشربه وكذلك فى جميع أحواله ثمّ صار الى
حال يتكلّم ويتحرّك فى الامور ويقبض ويبسط ويأكل و
يشرب ولا يستوحش ولا يجد مطالبة ولا يرى نقصا كما
كان يراه قبل، فقال هذه مسئلة حسنة فافهمها، فما أحوج
المريدين العمّال اليها، اعلم أنّ المريد الطالب للصدق فهو
عامل فى جميع أموره بالمراقبة لله عزّ وجلّ بالقيام على قلبه

وهمّه وجوارحه بالمحاسبة فهو جامع لهمّه حذرا من أن
يدخل فى همّه ما لا يعنيه حذرا من الغفلة فالحركات فى
ظاهر جوارحه بجوارحه تنقصه والهمم الداخلة عليه فى
قلبه تكدّر همّه فهو عند ذلك يتفرّغ من الحركات التى
ذكرت وإن كانت فى حقّ وبحقّ وذلك لما غلب على قلبه
من محبّته أن يكون ذكره دائما وهمّه واحدا فاذا دام على
ذلك تفطّن قلبه وصفت فكرته وسكن النور قلبه وقرب
من الله تعالى نغلب على قلبه وهمّه فعند ذلك يتكلّم و
القلب يغلى بالذكر لله عزّ وجلّ وقد كمنت فى سويداء
قلبه محبّة الله تعالى فهى لازمة للضمير لا تفارقه فمن
شأنه فى سرائره أن يكون ناعما بالمخاطبة لله الخفيّة و
المطالعة الشجيّة والمحادثة الشهيّة وهكذا يكون
فى أكله وشربه ونومه وكل حركاته لأنّ قرب الله تعالى
اذا تمكّن فى قلب العبد غلب على ما سواه (٣١) من باطن
عوارض الهمم وظاهر حركات الجوارح فعندها يكون العبد
ذاهبا وجائيا وآخذا ومعطيا والغالب على همّ ما قد ملك
ضميره من محبّة الله عزّ وجلّ وقربه، ألم ترنفسك أيها

المريد كيف تملّك قلبك أحيانا همّا من أمرالدنيا فيسلبك
عن كل شئ حتى يكد رعليك العيش فتكون ساهيا إلّا
عن ذلك حتى تفقد النوم، فأ مرالله عزّ وجلّ أحرى عند
العقلاء وأولى فعند ما ذكرنا صحبت العبد من الله عزّ و
جلّ العصمة فكان محفوظا من النقصان، فا فهم أيها السائل
ما يلقى اليك وتدبّره ينفعك إن شاء الله تعالى

وبعد فأعرض ما ذكرت لك على ما سألت عنه فإن
أجزاك وكان ما فقدت وما وجدت من جنس ما ذكرت
فاشكرالله تعالى يزيدك، ولا يخفى على العلماء ما يحدث
عندك فليس بين المريد وبين معلّمه رئاء إن شاء الله
تعالى، وإنّى بمؤدّب بصيرجهدى فى زماننا هذا وبالله التوفيق

تمّ كتاب الصدق للشيخ العارف أبى سعيد الخرّاز رحمه الله
ونفع بأنفاسه وسلّم عليه سلاما طيّبا مباركا فيه والحمد لله
وصلواته على محمّد وآله وصحبه وسلّم تسليما كثيرا كتبه
العبد الضعيف الفقير اسمعيل بن سودكين رفق الله به و
أخذ بيده ورحمه ورحم والديه وجميع المسلمين وحسبنا
الله ونعم الوكيل

مطبوعات

اداۂ اسلامی ریسرچ ایسوسی ایشن

ناشر

ہمفری ملفرڈ

اکسفورڈ یونیورسٹی پریس

لندن، نیویارک، بمبئی، کلکتہ، مدراس

مطبوعہ ایبل پریس بمبئی نمبر ۳